GW01044910

THE OFFICIAL WESTEROS COOKBOOK

RECIPES FROM

GAME OF THRONES™

AND

HOUSE OF THE DRAGON™

THE OFFICIAL

WESTEROS COOKBOOK

RECIPES FROM

GAME OF THRONES™

AND

HOUSE OF THE DRAGON™

CASSANDRA REEDER

JOANNE BOURNE

INSIGHT EDITIONS

SAN RAFAEL • LOS ANGELES • LONDON

CONTENTS

THE WESTERLANDS & THE IRON ISLANDS

THE STORMLANDS & THE REACH

DORNE

ACROSS THE NARROW SEA

INTRODUCTION

The two centuries from the accession of King Viserys I to the Great Council's election of Bran I the Broken were a golden age for the Westerosi table. Times were tumultuous, but the seasons were generally kind in those years and the harvests abundant. Noble houses had gold to spend, and merchants traded wine and spices across the seas, from Qarth, on the coast of the Jade Sea in the east, to the sunset island of the Arbor in the west.

Carts loaded with the land's bounty traveled by road from the fertile plains of the Reach all the way to the capital at King's Landing—a city that even brought in ice for its wells deep below the walls of the Red Keep.

In years when abundance waned from war and winter, farm and palace cooks were careful to obtain sufficient stocks and continued to hone their culinary skills, raising cooking to a high art in kitchens across the land.

On feast days and celebrations, noble tables were laden with plates of meats, sweet confections, and savories for guests to eat at will. Courses, when served, took the form of prestigious dishes cooked to impress, such as roast boar and live pigeon pie.

Larger towns prided themselves on their speciality goods. Fresh bread and small pastries were available from shops no bigger than a kitchen. Stallholders sold everything from meat to candies, fruit to wines.

Maesters and smallfolk alike knew the value of food as medicine, with potions, teas, and strong wines preserved and then prepared in times of need. Recipes were written down in noble houses or passed through the generations from memory as folk cures—and many saved lives.

The following pages contain recipes for food and drink collected from those centuries and presented by region, each with its own distinctive produce and cuisine. Within each region, recipes showcase a speciality dish or ingredient. The selections have been drawn from the kitchen books of the noble houses and gathered from the family traditions of farmhouses, inns, and tribes. Where necessary, they have been adapted for the modern cook, carefully crafted to retain the flavor of the Westerosi table.

CRUSTS, SEASONINGS, AND SAUCES

Westerosi recipes use three basic pastry crusts, each suited to particular pies: flaky crust, strong crust, and sweet crust. The recipes also make extensive use of herb and spice mixes and sauces for flavor and accompaniment. The ingredients and methods for preparing each type of crust are listed here for reference, with their use noted in the individual recipes that follow.

FLAKY CRUST

This flaky crust has a buttery flavor that complements both savory and sweet pies. This dough can be substituted with most premade pie doughs.

YIELD: TWO 9-INCH PIE CRUSTS OR 1 DOUBLE CRUST
PREP TIME: 30 MINUTES • REST TIME: 4 HOURS
DIFFICULTY: MODERATE

1 cup unsalted butter, diced and chilled

2½ cups all-purpose flour

¾ teaspoon fine salt

1 teaspoon granulated sugar

¼ cup ice water (or more as needed)

1. (Optional) Brown the butter: Add the butter to a small saucepan over medium heat. Cook until the butter melts and starts to foam on top. The butter should start to separate, becoming clear as the milk solids fall to the bottom of the saucepan and begin to brown. When the solids are medium brown (but not black or burnt) and the butter smells nutty and toasty, pour the butter into a heatproof storage container. Place the butter in the freezer for 10 minutes until it is once again very cold and firm; then dice for use in step 3.
2. In a large mixing bowl, add the flour, salt, and sugar. Whisk to combine.
3. Using clean hands, add in the pieces of butter; toss to coat the butter with the dry ingredients.
4. Using a pastry cutter or your hands, cut the butter into the flour until the mixture resembles coarse crumbs about the size of peas. This can also be done by pulsing the mixture in a food processor a couple times.
5. Add 1 tablespoon ice water at a time, mixing with a rubber spatula or your hands so that the dough holds together after each interval. You may need slightly less or slightly more than ¼ cup of ice water, depending on your location: Factors such as elevation, temperature, and humidity affect how much water is needed for the dough to come together. Test the dough by pinching it: If it holds together, it's ready.
6. Cut the dough in half, and shape into 2 discs. Wrap each disc in plastic wrap, and refrigerate for at least 4 hours. The dough can be stored in the refrigerator for up to 3 days or in the freezer for up to 3 months.
7. When you're ready to use the dough, remove it from the refrigerator and let it sit at room temperature for 15 minutes. Then roll it out and use as the individual recipe directs.

STRONG CRUST

This dough is made to hold its shape without support and to contain very wet fillings without too much leaking. It's best used for free-standing meat and savory pies. This dough cannot be substituted with premade pie dough.

YIELD: ONE 9-INCH RAISED FREE-STANDING PIE CRUST • PREP TIME: 20 MINUTES
REST TIME: NONE • DIFFICULTY: EASY

1 cup water

¾ cup lard, beef suet, or bacon grease (or use butter or shortening, if necessary)

4 cups all-purpose flour

1½ teaspoons fine salt

2 teaspoons granulated sugar

1. In a medium saucepan, heat the water and lard, stirring to combine the melted fat. Cover, and let come to a boil.
2. While the water and fat are coming to a boil, add the flour, salt, and sugar to a large heatproof mixing bowl. Stir to combine, and create a well in the center for the liquid.
3. When the water and fat have come to a boil, pour them into the well you created in the center of the flour mixture. Stir with a wooden spoon to combine until the mixture is cool enough to handle with your hands.
4. Turn out the dough mixture onto a lightly floured surface.
5. Knead the dough a few times with your hands; then cut off a third of the dough. Shape both pieces of dough into discs, and cover them with plastic wrap until you're ready to use them.
6. Use immediately, per the individual recipe directions. This crust cannot be refrigerated or frozen.

SWEET CRUST

This sweet crust is almost cookielike in flavor and texture, perfect for sweet tarts. It can be substituted with premade pie dough, if necessary—however, premade dough is less sweet and doesn't have the same soft, crumbly texture.

YIELD: TWO 9-INCH TART CRUSTS • PREP TIME: 20 MINUTES
REST TIME: 2 HOURS • DIFFICULTY: MODERATE

3 cups all-purpose flour

⅔ cup granulated sugar

1 teaspoon fine salt

1 teaspoon lemon zest (optional)

1 cup unsalted butter, diced and chilled

2 large egg yolks

1 teaspoon vanilla extract

1 to 3 tablespoons cold milk (as needed)

1. In a large mixing bowl, stir together the flour, sugar, salt, and lemon zest.
2. Add in the pieces of butter. Using clean hands, toss to coat.
3. Using a pastry cutter or your hands, cut the butter into the flour until the mixture resembles coarse crumbs about the size of peas. This can also be done by pulsing the mixture in a food processor.
4. In a small bowl, whisk together the egg yolks and the vanilla extract.
5. Add the egg yolk mixture to the flour mixture. Continue blending with the pastry cutter (or pulsing in the food processor) until the yolks are evenly incorporated and the mixture resembles a fine meal.
6. With a rubber spatula, add in the cold milk 1 tablespoon at a time until the mixture is moistened just enough to gather and mold into a smooth ball. Factors such as elevation, temperature, and humidity affect how much milk is needed for the dough to come together.
7. Cut the dough in half, and mold each portion into a smooth disc. Wrap with plastic wrap, and chill in the fridge for at least 2 hours. The dough can be stored in the refrigerator for up to 2 days or in the freezer for up to 2 months.
8. When you're ready to use the dough, remove it from the refrigerator and let it sit at room temperature for 15 minutes. Then roll it out and use it as the individual recipe directs.

WESTEROSI SWEET SPICE

YIELD: 8–12 SERVINGS • PREP TIME: 5 MINUTES
COOKING TIME: NONE • DIFFICULTY: EASY

3 tablespoons ground cinnamon
2 tablespoons ground ginger
1 tablespoon ground allspice
1 tablespoon ground nutmeg
1 teaspoon ground cloves
1 teaspoon ground mace

1. In a small bowl, add all the spices. Stir until well combined.
2. Use a funnel to transfer the spice mix to a spice jar or other sealable container.
3. Use as directed in the recipe.

Possible substitutes: Pumpkin spice, mixed spice, or apple pie spice

NORTHERN STRONG SPICES

YIELD: 6–8 SERVINGS • PREP TIME: 5 MINUTES
COOKING TIME: NONE • DIFFICULTY: EASY

1 tablespoon cinnamon
1 tablespoon black pepper
1 tablespoon ground ginger
1 teaspoon Tellicherry or white pepper
1 teaspoon mace
1 teaspoon ground grains of paradise (optional)

1. In a small bowl, add all the spices. Stir until well combined.
2. Use a funnel to transfer the spice mix to a spice jar or other sealable container.
3. Use as directed in the recipe.

Possible substitutes: Pumpkin spice or mixed spice, with additional pepper and ginger

OLD VALYRIAN BLEND

YIELD: 8–12 SERVINGS • PREP TIME: 5 MINUTES
COOKING TIME: NONE • DIFFICULTY: EASY

2 tablespoons garlic powder
2 tablespoons onion powder
1 tablespoon black pepper
1 tablespoon paprika
2 teaspoons dried thyme
½ teaspoon ground coriander
½ teaspoon dried parsley

1. In a small bowl, add all the spices. Stir until well combined.
2. Use a funnel to transfer the spice mix to a spice jar or other sealable container.
3. Use as directed in the recipe.

Possible substitutes: All-purpose seasoning

DORNISH SPICES

YIELD: 6–10 SERVINGS • PREP TIME: 5 MINUTES
COOKING TIME: NONE • DIFFICULTY: EASY

2 tablespoons ground cumin
2 tablespoons dried oregano
1 tablespoon garlic powder
2 teaspoons smoked paprika
1 teaspoon granulated lemon peel
½ teaspoon ground allspice
½ teaspoon ground cayenne (optional)

1. In a small bowl, add all the spices. Stir until well combined.
2. Use a funnel to transfer the spice mix to a spice jar or other sealable container.
3. Use as directed in the recipe.

Possible substitutes: Adobo seasoning, Sazón (Spanish blend) seasoning, or Mediterranean/ Greek seasoning

NOTE: *When substituting, pay attention to whether the seasoning blend contains salt. If it does, you will need less salt than the recipe calls for.*

ESSOSI SPICES

YIELD: 6–10 SERVINGS • PREP TIME: 5 MINUTES
COOKING TIME: NONE • DIFFICULTY: EASY

1 tablespoon ground turmeric
1 tablespoon ground cumin
1 tablespoon ground cinnamon
1 tablespoon ground coriander
1 tablespoon ground black pepper
1 teaspoon ground cloves
1 teaspoon ground cardamom (optional)

1. In a small bowl, add all the spices. Stir until well combined.
2. Use a funnel to transfer the spice mix to a spice jar or other sealable container.
3. Use as directed in the recipe.

Possible substitutes: Ras el hanout, baharat, berbere, or garam masala

NOTE: *When substituting, pay attention to whether the seasoning blend contains salt. If it does, you will need less salt than the recipe calls for.*

HOT PIE'S GRAVY

Serve this rich gravy as an accompaniment for roasted meats, meat pies, warm bread, and roasted vegetables.

YIELD: 8–12 SERVINGS • PREP TIME: 5 MINUTES
COOKING TIME: 20 MINUTES • DIFFICULTY: EASY

¼ cup unsalted butter or pan drippings
6 tablespoons all-purpose flour
3 cups beef broth
2 teaspoons beef bouillon base
2 teaspoons Worcestershire sauce
1 teaspoon garlic powder
2 teaspoons onion powder
1 bay leaf
Salt
Black pepper

1. Heat the butter or pan drippings in a medium saucepan over medium heat. When the butter has melted, add the flour. Whisk continuously until the mixture thickens and becomes a rich golden brown, about 7 to 8 minutes.
2. Slowly pour in the beef broth, a little at a time, while continuing to whisk until smooth. Whisk in the bouillon base, Worcestershire sauce, garlic powder, and onion powder; add the bay leaf. Taste, and adjust seasoning as desired.
3. While continuing to whisk, bring the mixture to a low boil; then reduce heat to a simmer. Allow the gravy to simmer, whisking occasionally, until it is thick and smooth, about 3 to 5 minutes.
4. Remove the bay leaf and season with salt and pepper, to taste.
5. Use immediately, or store in the refrigerator for 3 to 4 days or in the freezer for up to 3 months.

Dornish Spices
Westerosi Sweet Spice

KINGSWOOD BRAMBLE SAUCE

Serve this sauce as an accompaniment for white meats such as pork, duck, rabbit, and chicken, or with pork and poultry pies. It's also a good addition to cakes and creamy desserts.

YIELD: 6–10 SERVINGS • PREP TIME: 15 MINUTES
COOKING TIME: 15–20 MINUTES • DIFFICULTY: EASY

3 cups fresh or thawed frozen blackberries

1 cup pulp-free orange juice

½ cup dark brown sugar

½ cup balsamic vinegar

½ teaspoon fine salt

1 cinnamon stick (optional)

1. In a medium saucepan, add the blackberries, orange juice, brown sugar, and balsamic vinegar. Use a potato masher or a muddler to smash the berries.
2. Add the salt and cinnamon stick to the pot, if using. Bring the mixture to a simmer over medium heat; then turn the heat to low, and continue to simmer for 15 to 20 minutes, stirring occasionally to prevent burning, until the sauce has reduced by almost half.
3. Discard the cinnamon stick, and push the sauce through a fine mesh strainer into a bowl to remove the seeds. You can use a spoon to stir and press the seeds into the strainer to release any lingering liquid, but don't stress about getting every last drop.
4. Use immediately, or transfer the sauce to a sealable heatproof storage container, such as a mason jar, and refrigerate until ready to serve. It can be refrigerated for up to 2 weeks and frozen for up to 4 months.

NORTHERN ALE PRESERVES

This spiced savory-sweet condiment makes an excellent companion to meat and meat pies as well as a good pairing with breads, cured meats, and cheeses.

YIELD: 8–12 SERVINGS • PREP TIME: 20 MINUTES
COOKING TIME: 1 HOUR • DIFFICULTY: EASY

4 to 5 apples, peeled, cored, and cut into ¼-inch cubes

¾ cup raisins

1 white onion, finely chopped

1 garlic clove, minced

1 tablespoon minced fresh ginger

1 tablespoon whole yellow mustard seeds

½ teaspoon cracked black pepper

½ teaspoon ground cinnamon

¼ teaspoon ground allspice

½ cup apple cider vinegar

½ cup stout beer or porter

½ cup dark brown sugar

1. In a large saucepan, combine the apples, raisins, onion, ginger, mustard seeds, and spices. Cook over medium-low heat, stirring frequently, until the apples have softened and are tender, about 15 to 20 minutes.
2. Add in the vinegar, stout/porter, and brown sugar, and stir until the sugar dissolves completely.
3. Raise the temperature to medium high, and bring to a low boil; then turn the heat back to low. Let simmer on very low heat, uncovered, for about 1 hour, or until thickened to a jam-like consistency. Stir occasionally, to prevent any burning on the bottom.
4. Let the mixture cool for 10 minutes; then ladle into a sterilized mason jar, and secure with a lid. Store in the fridge for up to 2 months.

MEEREENESE HERB SAUCE

Meereenese Herb Sauce adds a bright and zesty flavor to any roasted or grilled meat or fish, as well as savory pies and grilled or roasted vegetables.

YIELD: 6–8 SERVINGS • PREP TIME: 15 MINUTES
COOKING TIME: NONE • DIFFICULTY: EASY

1 packed cup fresh cilantro leaves, with tender stems
1 packed cup fresh flat-leaf parsley, with tender stems
1 packed cup fresh mint leaves
1 shallot, roughly chopped
2 garlic cloves
1 Fresno chile (or use red pepper flakes)
¾ cup extra virgin olive oil
¼ cup lemon juice
1 teaspoon smoked paprika
¾ teaspoon ground cumin
½ teaspoon lemon zest
Salt
Black pepper

1. Use a mortar and pestle to pound the fresh herbs, shallot, garlic, and Fresno chile into fine pieces, or use a sharp knife to dice them into very small pieces. Alternatively, pulse them in a food processor with the rest of the ingredients; if using this method, however, be careful not to overprocess—some texture is preferred.
2. Combine the ingredients in a small mixing bowl. Taste, and adjust seasonings as desired.
3. Use immediately, or refrigerate for up to 2 weeks or freeze for up to 2 months.

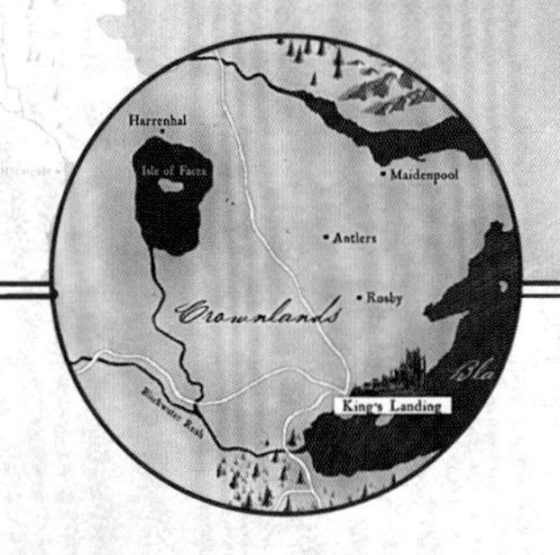

THE CROWNLANDS

The capital region of the Crownlands lies to the east of Westeros, its borders forming the shape of a hungry dragon's mouth snapping at the islands in Blackwater Bay. Its lakes, rivers, forests, and fields provided food for the populace, much of it destined for the noble tables of King's Landing. What could not be farmed or hunted was imported by ship or cart, and the cooks of the capital had the finest Westerosi ingredients for their superior dishes.

V • YIELD: 4 TO 6 SERVINGS • PREP TIME: 5 MINUTES
COOKING TIME: 35 MINUTES • DIFFICULTY: EASY

PRINCELING'S PORRIDGE

The porridge made in the kitchens of the Red Keep was a light, spiced wheaten mix made with egg yolk and cream. Served with butter and honey, it was considered in royal circles to be the "breakfast of kings."

2 cups water

½ teaspoon fine salt

1 cup bulgur or cracked wheat

½ cup currants or raisins (optional)

1 cup half-and-half or whole milk

2 egg yolks, lightly beaten

1 to 2 teaspoons Westerosi Sweet Spice (page 11)

¼ teaspoon saffron (optional)

Unsalted butter, for serving

Honey for serving

Grated nutmeg, for serving (optional)

1. Bring the water and salt to a boil in a medium saucepan over medium-high heat.
2. Add the bulgur or cracked wheat, and stir.
3. Reduce heat to low, and cover. Allow to simmer for 15 to 20 minutes or until the water is almost completely absorbed and the wheat is cooked and softened.
4. Stir in the currants or raisins and cover, keeping the stove on low heat.
5. In a separate bowl, whisk together the half-and-half, egg yolks, and spices.
6. Pour the cream/egg yolk mixture into the cooked bulgur or cracked wheat, and stir to combine. Continue to simmer on low heat until the porridge is very thick about 10 to 15 minutes.
7. Serve the porridge warm with butter and honey. Add a sprinkle of cinnamon or nutmeg on top.

"*This morning he insisted on eating porridge with his hands.*"

OTTO HIGHTOWER

V • YIELD: 12 TO 18 CAKES • PREP TIME: 30 MINUTES
COOKING TIME: 30 MINUTES • DIFFICULTY: MODERATE

RHAENYRA'S LEMON CAKES

The pâtissiers of Westeros each had their own special recipe for lemon cake—some sweet, some sharp, some syrupy, some tart—and each swore that their confections were the original and best.

The secret ingredient in these exquisite lemon wheels was olive oil, the finest Dorne could provide. The cakes were baked bottom up and overturned to serve, revealing a fine slice of candied lemon. These cakes were reputed to be a favorite of the young Rhaenyra Targaryen and were popular in the early years of King Viserys's reign.

TOPPING

½ cup unsalted butter, melted

½ cup granulated sugar

2 to 3 Meyer lemons, sliced very thin (about ⅛ inch thick)

CAKES

1 cup high-quality olive oil

3 large eggs, lightly beaten

1 cup granulated sugar

1 teaspoon vanilla extract

2 tablespoons lemon zest

½ cup lemon juice

2 cups all-purpose flour

¾ teaspoon fine salt

½ teaspoon baking powder

½ teaspoon baking soda

½ teaspoon turmeric

1 cup whole milk

1. Preheat the oven to 325°F. Generously grease 2 standard 12-hole muffin tins.
2. To make the topping: Distribute the melted butter for the topping among all depressions of the muffin tin, filling the full 12 holes of one tin and 4 to 6 holes in the other tin. Sprinkle the sugar for the topping into each depression. Add 1 thin lemon slice to the bottom of each depression. Set aside.
3. To make the cakes: In a large mixing bowl, whisk together the olive oil, eggs, and sugar.
4. Add the vanilla, lemon zest, and lemon juice; whisk to combine.
5. In a separate medium mixing bowl, sift together the flour, salt, baking powder, baking soda, and turmeric.
6. Alternating with the milk, add the dry ingredients to the wet ingredients in 2 to 3 additions, stirring just enough to combine. Be careful not to overmix; the batter should be satiny and smooth but not thick or gluey.
7. Distribute the batter into each depression of the muffin tin, as evenly as possible.
8. Bake for 25 to 30 minutes or until a toothpick inserted into the center of one of the cakes comes out clean.
9. Remove the cakes from the oven, and allow to cool for 10 minutes while still in the tin. Gently remove the cakes from the tin, using a knife around the edges, if necessary. Flip the cakes upside down so that the lemon slice is on top. Allow the cakes to cool completely on a wire rack. Serve slightly warm or at room temperature.

NOTE: *If some of the bottoms of the cakes are too round to lay flat when flipped, cut off the rounded part with a sharp knife.*

“*I want to fly with you on dragon back, see the great wonders across the Narrow Sea, and eat only cake.*”

RHAENYRA TARGARYEN

STUFFED "DRAGON" EGGS

The "dragon eggs" of the Crownlands feast days at the height of the Targaryen reign were made from the eggs of hens, geese, or ducks that were hard boiled, marinated, and dressed with herbs and spices. The marinade added flavor and showed the chefs' artistry: Steeping the broken eggs in the liquor created a craquelure "scale" pattern on the white, in honor of the real dragons of Westeros.

MARINADE (OPTIONAL)

4 black tea bags

1 cinnamon stick

1 teaspoon whole cloves

1 teaspoon black peppercorns

⅔ cup soy sauce

¼ cup dark brown sugar

1 teaspoon red pepper flakes (optional)

2 garlic cloves, minced

EGGS

1 dozen eggs, hard boiled

½ cup labneh, crème fraîche, or sour cream

1 to 2 tablespoons harissa paste or hot pepper sauce of your choice, plus more for garnish

1 teaspoon Old Valyrian Blend (page 11)

1 teaspoon Dornish Spices (page 11)

1 teaspoon turmeric

Salt

Black pepper

1 to 2 teaspoons lemon juice

Smoked paprika, for garnish

Chopped chives, mint, and/or cilantro, for garnish

1. If using marinade: Marinade the eggs, steep the black tea bags in 2 cups of boiled water, along with the cinnamon stick, cloves, and peppercorns. Remove the tea bags after 7 to 8 minutes, and let cool while the spices continue to steep. Once cooled to room temperature, remove the tea bags and spices (or keep the spices in for a stronger spiced flavor) and add the liquid to a large mixing bowl. Whisk the tea mixture and remaining marinade ingredients together. Using a spoon, gently crack the shells of the eggs all around the surface, to create a pattern and let the marinade steep through. Place the eggs in the marinade, making sure they are completely covered. Cover, and refrigerate for 1 to 3 days. The longer the eggs marinate, the stronger the pattern and flavor will be.
2. Peel the eggs and slice a small piece off the bottoms so that they are able to stand upright. Slice the top third off of each. Optionally, set the tops aside.
3. With a small spoon, remove the yolks and transfer them to a large bowl, taking care to not tear the eggs in the process. Mash the yolks with a fork. Add the labneh, crème fraîche, or sour cream; the harissa or hot sauce; spices; and lemon juice. Stir until fully combined and smooth. Taste, and adjust the seasoning to your liking.
4. Transfer the yolk mixture to a piping bag or a plastic bag with a corner snipped off. Pipe the yolk mixture into the egg bottoms.
5. Garnish with additional hot pepper sauce, smoked paprika, and chives. Arrange the eggs on a serving platter. Partially cover with the reserved egg tops, if desired. Refrigerate until ready to serve.

V, V+*, GF • YIELD: 6 SERVINGS • PREP TIME: 15 MINUTES
COOKING TIME: 1 HOUR • DIFFICULTY: EASY

POACHED PEARS

The fragrant, wine-infused sweet course of poached pears graced many noble tables in King's Landing. The favorite royal recipe used crisp, flawless pears from the orchards of the Reach, harvested and dispatched by cart to the kitchens of the Red Keep, where they were preserved and prepared for feast days with a spiced caramelized sauce. The rich infusion heightened the soft pear flavor, with the whole dish maturing in depth in the days after steeping.

2 to 3 cups sweet wine or fruit juice

1 to 2 oranges, sliced

¼ cup honey

¼ cup brown sugar

1 vanilla bean pod, split (or use 1 teaspoon vanilla extract)

2 cinnamon sticks

5 whole cloves

5 whole allspice berries

1 star anise

2-inch slice fresh ginger

2 cardamom pods, lightly crushed (optional)

6 to 8 ripe but firm pears, ideally Bosc or Anjou

1. To a large saucepan, add the wine, oranges, honey, brown sugar, vanilla seeds or vanilla extract, and spices. Make sure there is enough liquid to submerge at least half of the pears: Add more wine or juice, if necessary. Bring the mixture to a low boil over medium-high heat, stirring until the sugar and honey dissolve.
2. While the wine is heating, peel the pears. Discard the skins; keep the stems on. Use a spoon to core the pears from the bottom.
3. Reduce heat to medium-low, and arrange the pears on their sides in the saucepan. Simmer the pears for 15 to 20 minutes; then rotate them so that the other side is submerged, and simmer for another 15 to 20 minutes until both sides of the pears are nicely colored and the flesh is soft.
4. Using a slotted spoon, remove and discard the orange slices. Gently remove the pears from the liquid, and set them aside.
5. Increase heat to high, and boil until the liquid reduces to about ¾ cup and turns slightly syrupy, about 10 to 15 minutes. Remove the saucepan from heat. Strain out the whole spices using a mesh strainer, and discard them.
6. When the pears are cool enough to serve, plate them in the syrup, facing upright.

YIELD: 6 TO 8 SERVINGS • PREP TIME: 40 MINUTES
COOKING TIME: 4 HOURS (MOSTLY IDLE) • DIFFICULTY: ADVANCED

LARYS STRONG'S MEAT PIE

The kitchens of the Red Keep prepared outstanding meat dishes, among them a wine-braised short rib pie. This slow-cooked beef in a rich meat sauce, enfolded in a buttery pie crust, was a castle favorite, made in a large dish for a family supper or in small ramekins for individual dining.

3 pounds bone-in beef short ribs
Salt
Black pepper
¼ cup flour
1 star anise
6 sprigs fresh thyme
4 sprigs fresh rosemary
2 bay leaves
2 tablespoons oil
2 tablespoons unsalted butter
8 shallots, chopped
6 garlic cloves, minced
1 bottle (750 mL) dry red wine
1 tablespoon Old Valyrian Blend (page 11)
2 to 4 cups beef broth
1 tablespoon potato or corn starch
½ Flaky Pie Crust (page 9)
1 egg, lightly beaten, for washing
Sea salt, for finishing

This pie can also be baked in individual 9- to 12-ounce ramekins, if desired.

1. Preheat the oven to 300°F.
2. Season the meat with salt and pepper, to taste, and then toss the ribs in the flour to coat. Set aside.
3. Cut a 3- to 4-inch piece of kitchen twine, and loop the string through the center of the star anise. Then use the twine to tie together the thyme, rosemary, and bay leaves. This will make it easier to remove all the herbs later.
4. Heat the oil in a Dutch oven or heavy-bottomed pot over medium-high heat. Brown the meat for 3 to 4 minutes on each side. You may need to work in batches to avoid crowding the pan. Remove the browned meat, and set it aside.
5. Melt the butter over medium-high heat in the same Dutch oven you used to cook the meat. Add the shallots, and cook, stirring occasionally, for 2 to 3 minutes. Add the garlic, and cook for another minute until fragrant. Add a splash of wine, and use a wooden spoon to scrape up any browned bits on the bottom of the pan.
6. Add the beef back to the Dutch oven, along with the herb bundle, Old Valyrian Blend, wine, and 2 cups of broth. Add more broth as needed to cover the beef, up to 4 cups.
7. Transfer the pot to the preheated oven. Allow it to cook for 3 hours or until the meat is fork tender and the liquid has reduced significantly. Be sure to check on it periodically and stir, to prevent burning on the bottom.
8. Remove the herb bundle, and use a wooden spoon or a fork to remove the meat from the bones. Stir to break up the meat and coat it with the gravy. Discard the bones. Ideally, the liquid will have reduced to a gravy-like consistency. If it hasn't yet, put the Dutch oven on the stove over medium heat. Whisk the potato starch with 2 tablespoons of water, and add it to the pot, cooking and stirring until the gravy has thickened, about 3 to 4 minutes.

Continued on page 28

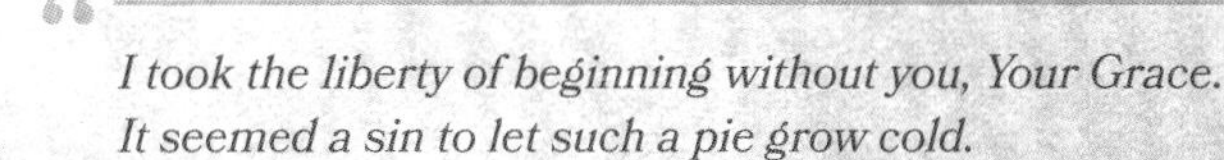

*I took the liberty of beginning without you, Your Grace.
It seemed a sin to let such a pie grow cold.*

LARYS STRONG

9. Transfer the filling to a shallow 2-quart baking dish. Roll out the dough on a lightly floured surface to about ⅛ inch thick. Carefully transfer the dough to the baking dish, placing it over the filling, and trim it, leaving a slight overhang. Tuck the edges under, and crimp them with your fingers. Cut a few slits in the crust, to vent steam. Brush the entire surface of the top crust with egg wash, and sprinkle with sea salt.
10. Place the baking dish on a rimmed baking sheet, and bake the pie until the filling is bubbling and the crust is golden brown, 50 to 60 minutes. You may need to drape a sheet of aluminum foil over the pie halfway through cooking, to prevent the edges from burning.
11. Let cool for 5 to 10 minutes before serving.

GF • YIELD: 4 SERVINGS • PREP TIME: 15 MINUTES
COOKING TIME: 30 MINUTES • DIFFICULTY: MODERATE

ROAST DUCK

The duck hunts of the Riverlands took place in fall and early winter. Smallfolk used traps or nets with some efficiency to nab birds, but young squires saw hunting as a chance to hone their combat skills: They used dogs to chase prey from the waters at first light and felled birds in flight using bows and arrows or even falcons. The ducks were packed in straw and ice and sent in carts to the towns, where citizens enjoyed them served plain, seasoned, seared and roasted, or accompanied by a rich sauce.

4 boneless skin-on duck breasts (6 to 8 ounces each)

1 tablespoon Old Valyrian Blend (page 11)

1 to 2 teaspoons Northern Strong Spices (page 11)

1 teaspoon fine salt (or to taste)

2 to 4 tablespoons oil, for searing

Kingswood Bramble Sauce (page 14), for serving

1. Preheat the oven to 400°F. If the duck breasts are not at room temperature, defrost them (if frozen) and let them sit on the counter for a while. Pat the duck breasts dry with a paper towel.
2. With a sharp knife, score the skin of the duck breasts in a criss-cross pattern.
3. Thoroughly rub the duck breasts with the seasoning and salt, spreading it through all the nooks and crannies. Before adding salt, be sure to check whether your duck breasts have been premarinated; sometimes duck breasts are packaged with a salt solution.
4. Heat a heavy-bottomed cast-iron or other oven-proof skillet over medium heat until the pan is hot.
5. Place the duck breasts in the hot skillet, fat side down, for about 7 to 8 minutes.
6. Use tongs to flip the duck breasts so the fat side is facing up, and place the skillet in the oven. Roast for 10 to 12 minutes, or until the breasts are medium rare (pink in the middle) or medium (slightly pink in the center), with an internal temperature of around 135° to 140°F.
7. Remove the skillet from the oven, and let the breasts rest for 10 minutes.
8. Slice the breasts into ¼- or ½-inch slices, and serve over Kingswood Bramble Sauce.

"*Dare I say it is a matter of taste? I prefer roast duck to goose. I cannot say why.*"

RHAENYRA TARGARYEN

GF • YIELD: 4 SERVINGS • PREP TIME: 30 MINUTES
COOKING TIME: 90 MINUTES • DIFFICULTY: MODERATE

HONEYED GAME BIRDS

Tender young hens, buttered, roasted, and basted with a honey syrup, were served hot with gravy or a tart bramble sauce.

Game birds were often prepared for feast tables in King's Landing, especially after large celebratory hunts. Kitchen notes show them to have been at the table of Rhaenyra Targaryen and Laenor Velaryon's prewedding feast, an event remembered for the tragic death of Joffrey Lonmouth, Laenor's lover, at the hand of Ser Criston Cole.

4 Cornish game hens

3 to 4 teaspoons fine salt (or to taste)

4 teaspoons Old Valyrian Blend (page 14)

2 teaspoons fresh thyme, chopped

2 teaspoons fresh oregano, chopped

4 sprigs fresh rosemary

4 shallots, roughly chopped

1 small orange, sliced

8 garlic cloves, roughly chopped

6 tablespoons unsalted butter (divided)

½ cup honey, loosened

½ cup pulp-free orange juice

1. Pat the hens dry with paper towels. Season the hens inside and out with salt, Old Valyrian Blend, and chopped fresh thyme and oregano. Set aside.
2. Stuff the cavities of the birds with the rosemary, shallots, sliced orange, and garlic. Tie the legs of the birds together using some kitchen twine.
3. Preheat the oven to 400°F. Place the birds in a shallow roasting pan or cast-iron skillet with breasts facing up, and add ½ tablespoon butter on top of each. Transfer the hens to the oven, and roast for 30 to 35 minutes.
4. While the hens are roasting, add the honey, orange juice, and remaining butter to a small saucepan. Cook over medium-high heat, stirring occasionally. Reduce the sauce until it appears syrupy, about 10 to 15 minutes.
5. When the hens have been roasting for 30 to 35 minutes, baste them with half the sauce, reserving the remaining half for later.
6. Put the hens back in the oven, and roast for another 10 to 15 minutes or until the internal temperature of the largest bird reads 160°F in the thickest part of the thigh.
7. Remove the hens from the oven, and drizzle or brush them with the remaining sauce.
8. Allow the hens to rest for 10 minutes before serving.

PAIRS WELL WITH:

Hot Pie's Gravy (page 12) or Kingswood Bramble Sauce (page 14)

V, V+*, GF • YIELD: 2 TO 4 SERVINGS • PREP TIME: 15 MINUTES
REST TIME: 3 HOURS • DIFFICULTY: EASY

MILK OF THE POPPY

The Maesters of the Citadel had a soothing drink for the weak and infirm, a recipe known to all Maesters in the Seven Kingdoms. The potion contained distilled essence of the poppy and was sometimes flavored with saffron, dates, and honey. It was served warm or chilled and could be diluted with wine, tea, or brandy.

Such was the sedative effect that some—most notably, brothers Jaime and Tyrion Lannister—chose to endure pain and retain their ability to think clearly, knowing that the potion risked hindering their judgment.

1 cup poppy seeds

3 cups filtered warm water

1 tablespoon vanilla extract

1 to 2 dates, pitted

¼ teaspoon saffron or turmeric powder (optional)

2 tablespoons honey (or to taste)

¼ teaspoon fine salt

Ground cinnamon or Westerosi Sweet Spice (optional) (page 11)

2 to 4 ounces vanilla or regular brandy, for serving (optional)

1. Add the poppy seeds to a mason jar, and cover with warm water. Put on the lid, and let the poppy seeds soak for at least 3 hours (or soak them in the fridge overnight).
2. Strain, and add the seeds to a blender, along with the 3 cups of filtered water, vanilla, dates, saffron or turmeric, honey, salt, and cinnamon or spices (to taste).
3. Blend for 2 to 4 minutes or until the seeds release milk and the water turns a yellowish white.
4. Strain the mixture through a cheesecloth into a bowl, squeezing to extract as much of the milk as possible.
5. Taste and adjust the sweetness level as desired. Serve warm or chilled, or mixed with 2 ounces of brandy per serving cup. The drink can also be added to teas and other hot brewed drinks or sweet dessert wines.
6. Store any extra milk of the poppy in a mason jar or a capped bottle in the refrigerator for up to 2 weeks. Shake before serving.

"*It is they who keep him addled on milk of the poppy while the Hightowers warm his throne.*"

RHAENYRA TARGARYEN

GF • YIELD: 10 TO 12 SERVINGS • PREP TIME: 45 MINUTES
REST TIME: 6 HOURS - OVERNIGHT • COOKING TIME: 4 HOURS • DIFFICULTY: ADVANCED

ROASTED BOAR

Pigs, both wild and farmed, were a Westerosi staple, used nose to tail by farm and castle cooks. The most coveted part of the pig was the belly. With its thick mantle of fat, pig belly was rolled with garlic, shallots, apples, leeks, and herbs; secured with twine; and slow roasted until the skin crisped. Such preparation heightened the already flavorful meat.

5- to 6-pound slab of boneless, skin-on pork belly

2 tablespoons apple cider vinegar

2 tablespoons neutral oil, plus more for greasing

4 teaspoons salt, divided (or to taste)

2 tablespoons Old Valyrian Blend (page 11)

10 garlic cloves, minced

3 to 4 shallots, chopped

1 to 2 apples, peeled, cored, and sliced

Fresh herbs (such as rosemary, thyme, and oregano)

1 teaspoon baking powder

PAIRS WELL WITH:

Kingswood Bramble Sauce (page 14, Northern Ale Preserves (page 14) or Hot Pie's Gravy (page 12).

1. Lay out paper towels on a large tray or baking sheet. Place the pork on the paper towels, belly skin side down. Use a sharp knife to score the meat diagonally about ¼ to ½ inch deep (make sure you're not going through all the way to the skin); then repeat, going the opposite direction, to create diamond-shaped scores.
2. Use additional paper towels to pat the pork completely dry. Brush the pork with the vinegar on all sides, and let it sit for 10 minutes. Rub the oil over the entire surface of the pork, front and back. Rub the meat side with 2 teaspoons of the salt and the Old Valyrian Blend, making sure to rub the seasoning into the crevices and over the sides of the slab. (You'll season the skin side later.)
3. Arrange the garlic, shallots, apple slices, and herbs on the meat.
4. Cut about 6 strings of kitchen twine long enough to wrap twice around the pork belly. Place the strings under the meat in 2- to 3-inch intervals.
5. Roll the pork tightly into a log around the fillings, and secure with the twine, starting with the two outermost strings. The twine should be tied tight enough to keep everything in place, but not so tight that the pork is bulging a lot.
6. In a small bowl, combine the remaining 2 teaspoons of salt with the baking powder.
7. Pat the pork skin dry with paper towels once more. Rub the salt and baking powder mixture over the entire surface of the pork skin.
8. Wrap the roll tightly in plastic wrap, and let it sit in the fridge for at least 3 hours, or up to 3 days. When you're ready, remove the pork from the refrigerator and allow it to come to room temperature for 2 to 3 hours before roasting.

Continued on page 36

> *I want the funeral feast to be the biggest the Kingdoms ever saw. And I want everyone to taste the boar that got me.*
>
> ROBERT BARATHEON

9. Preheat the oven to 300°F. Prepare a roasting pan by lining the bottom with aluminum foil and placing a grill rack in the center. Spray or brush the grill rack with oil.
10. Loosely cover the exposed meat on the sides of the roll with aluminum foil, but make sure all the skin is still exposed.
11. Place the roasting pan on the lower rack of the oven, and roast until a knife inserted in the center meets little to no resistance after it has penetrated the skin layer, approximately 3 to 4 hours. Baste the pork with pan drippings every half-hour or so, starting at around 90 minutes.
12. Increase the oven heat to 500°F, and cook for 5 to 10 minutes at this temperature until the skin crisps and blisters. If the bottom isn't getting crisped, rotate the pork roll, and continue to cook at this temperature for another 5 to 10 minutes.
13. Allow the pork to rest for 20 minutes. To serve, slice into 1-inch-thick disks with a sharp, serrated knife. It's best to cut off slices only as you are serving instead of cutting them all at once. Pour Kingswood Bramble Sauce over the slices, or serve it on the side. You can also serve the boar with Northern Ale Preserves or Hot Pie's Gravy.

V • YIELD: 12 TARTS • PREP TIME: 30 MINUTES
COOKING TIME: 90 MINUTES • DIFFICULTY: MODERATE

BURNT LEMON TARTS

King's Landing street traders sold some of the best food in the capital. The finest baked goods were found here, made by the artisan bakers who had traded there for generations. The lemon tarts—made of rich citrus custard and light, flaky pastry—cost just coppers and were sold individually or by the dozen.

Butter, for greasing

1 Sweet Crust (page 10) or one 14-ounce package frozen puff pastry, thawed

¾ cup granulated sugar

½ cup water

1 cinnamon stick

Peel of 1 large lemon

1 cup whole milk

½ cup heavy cream

1 large egg

5 large egg yolks

1 tablespoon vanilla extract

3 tablespoons potato or corn starch

1 tablespoon lemon zest

1. Generously grease 12 mini pie tins or a muffin tin with butter.
2. Roll out the Sweet Crust or pastry onto a lightly floured work surface. Cut the pastry into 12 equal rounds using a large cookie cutter, or use a wide-mouth mason jar.
3. Line the pie tins with the pastry, pushing it into the sides and bottom of the tins. If using a muffin tin, push each piece of pastry down and up into the sides of the muffin holes until evenly distributed. Place the tins in the refrigerator until ready to use.
4. In a small saucepan over medium heat, add the sugar, water, cinnamon stick, and lemon peel. Bring to a simmer. Allow to simmer for 3 minutes; then remove from heat, and set aside to cool and infuse.
5. In a separate saucepan, heat the milk and cream over medium heat. Allow the mixture to come to a simmer; then remove from heat, and set aside to cool.
6. In a large mixing bowl, add the egg, egg yolks, vanilla, potato or corn starch, and lemon zest. Whisk vigorously until smooth.
7. While whisking vigorously, slowly introduce the hot milk mixture to the egg mixture.
8. Return the egg and milk mixture to the larger saucepan, and cook over medium-low heat. Whisk continually until the mixture thickens enough to coat the back of a spoon, around 3 to 4 minutes.
9. Add in the cooled sugar syrup through a mesh strainer, whisking continuously. Discard the cinnamon stick and lemon peel. Continue to cook until the custard thickens back up to a runny, puddinglike consistency. Remove the custard from heat, and set aside.
10. Preheat the oven to 475°F.
11. Take the pastry-lined tins out of the refrigerator. Pour the custard into each pie tin or muffin hole until each one is approximately three-quarters full. Bake for 20 to 25 minutes or until golden and browned on top.
12. Let cool for 15 minutes. Then remove the tarts from the tins, and serve warm.

> *Can I have one? A lemon one—or any of them.*
>
> ARYA STARK

YIELD: 8 SERVINGS • PREP TIME: 30 MINUTES
COOKING TIME: 90 MINUTES • DIFFICULTY: MODERATE

SHAE'S FISH PIE

Hot smoked salmon and leek tart was a castle favorite, yet it divided opinion in the capital among those who were fond of fish and those who weren't. The fish lovers praised the tart's crumbly crust, its spindles of flaked pink salmon, and the subtle cheese flavor of the cream sauce. Variations were served throughout the city.

½ Flaky Crust (page 9)

2 tablespoons unsalted butter

1 leek, white and light green parts only, sliced

1 small bunch thin asparagus, trimmed and snapped in half

½ cup English peas, shelled

Salt

Black pepper

4 large eggs

½ cup heavy cream

2 teaspoons Old Valyrian Blend (page 11)

1 teaspoon lemon zest

6 ounces hot smoked salmon, flaked

4 ounces goat cheese or brie (or soft cheese of your choice), crumbled or thinly sliced

2 tablespoons fresh herbs (dill, chives, tarragon, parsley), chopped

1. Preheat the oven to 400°F. Grease a 10-inch fluted tart pan with a removable bottom or a 9-inch pie tin.
2. Roll out the pie dough to 12 inches round and ⅛ inch thick. Carefully transfer the round to the tart tin; press it into the bottom and sides of the tin, and trim any excess.
3. Melt the butter over medium heat in a medium skillet. When the pan is hot and the butter has melted, add the leek: Sauté, stirring occasionally, for 4 to 5 minutes or until the leek softens. Add the asparagus and the peas, season with salt and pepper to taste, and cook for 2 more minutes or until just heated through. Remove the skillet from heat, and set aside.
4. Line the pie crust with parchment paper, and fill with pie weights, dried beans, or uncooked rice. Bake in the oven for 10 minutes. Then remove the parchment paper and weights, and bake for another 10 minutes. Remove the crust, and reduce the oven's heat to 325°F.
5. In a small mixing bowl, whisk together the eggs, cream, Old Valyrian Blend, lemon zest, and salt and pepper to taste.
6. Spread the leek mixture over the bottom of the pie, followed by the salmon, cheese, and herbs. Pour the egg and cream mixture over everything.
7. Place the pie on a rimmed baking sheet, and bake for 30 to 35 minutes until set.
8. Allow to cool for 15 to 20 minutes before slicing and serving.

NOTE: *If you're absolutely not a fisherman, try this pie with bacon or ham instead of smoked salmon.*

> *Strange things do happen. You should taste her fish pie.*
>
> TYRION LANNISTER

MULLED WINE

The ancient mix of wine and honey was a revered drink in Westeros, not just for its intoxicating properties, but also for its medicinal value. The cooks of the Red Keep simmered the wine and honey mix with the juices of oranges and spices shipped from the trading city of Qarth. Cinnamon was said to be good for the heart and the blood, cloves helped with coughs, allspice eased aches and pains, and star anise lessened headaches. Often drunk warm as a dessert or nightcap, mulled wine reputedly ensured a dreamless sleep.

1 (750 mL) bottle red wine

2 cups pulp-free orange juice

¼ cup honey

3 cinnamon sticks

5 whole cloves

5 whole allspice berries

2 bay leaves

1 whole star anise

Seeds from a vanilla pod (or use 1 teaspoon vanilla extract)

1 small orange, sliced

1 lemon or lime, sliced

1 cardamom pod, lightly crushed (optional)

Pinch of saffron (optional)

1. Add the wine, orange juice, and honey to a Dutch oven or similar large pot, and stir to combine.
2. Add the remaining ingredients, and bring to a low simmer over medium-high heat—but don't let it boil.
3. Reduce heat to low, and let simmer gently, uncovered, for 30 minutes. Taste, and adjust sweetness, adding more honey if desired.
4. To serve, ladle into mugs and garnish with the lemon and lime slices and cinnamon sticks.

> *Will you take a cup with me? I find that mulled wine helps me sleep.*
>
> TYRION LANNISTER

YIELD: 10 TO 12 SERVINGS • PREP TIME: 90 MINUTES
COOKING TIME: 3 HOURS • REST TIME: 2 HOURS • DIFFICULTY: ADVANCED

PIGEON PIE

While some Westerosi cooks made pies from spiced pigeon, hunted from field and forest or raised in the dovecots of noble estates, the cooks of King's Landing favored chicken, considering it a sweeter, more meaty bird.

Pigeon pies were also created in the capital as showpieces for feast days, such as the pie made for the wedding of King Joffrey Baratheon and his bride, Margaery Tyrell. This giant coroneted pastry confection embellished with bas relief vines contained a flock of live pigeons, awaiting release at the skilful strike of a sword. King Joffrey was known to be hasty with his blade, and several birds died at his hand. The King himself perished at the feast, killed not by the pie, as first believed, but by wine poisoned with an amethyst crystal known as "the strangler."

1½ pounds boneless squab breasts or boneless, skinless chicken thighs

Salt

Black pepper

1 tablespoon oil

2 tablespoons unsalted butter, plus more for greasing

16 ounces fresh mushrooms

3 shallots, chopped

6 garlic cloves, minced, divided

2 tablespoons fresh herbs (such as thyme, sage, and rosemary), chopped

1½ pounds ground chicken or turkey

½ cup plain bread crumbs, plus more for sprinkling

1 medium egg, lightly beaten, plus more for washing

1. Liberally season the squab or chicken thighs with salt and pepper. Heat the oil in a skillet over high heat. Once the oil is hot, brown the meat for about 1 to 2 minutes per side. The meat should have some color on the outside but not be fully cooked through. Remove the squab or chicken from the skillet, and set aside.
2. In the same skillet over medium heat, add the butter and let it melt. Add the mushrooms, the shallots, half the minced garlic, and the herbs. Sauté until the mushrooms and shallots have browned and softened and the mushrooms have reduced in size by half, about 6 to 7 minutes. Remove the skillet from heat, and set aside.
3. In a medium mixing bowl, mix together the ground chicken, bread crumbs, egg, pancetta or bacon, currants or raisins, spices, and remaining minced garlic. Set aside.
4. Preheat the oven to 375°F. Grease a 10-inch springform pan with butter.
5. Roll out the larger portion of the dough to an 18-inch circle ¼ inch thick. Reserve some dough for decor. Press the dough into the rounded corners of the pan so that you have a clear bottom of the pie with tall edges around the springform. Trim any excess, and set it aside for decor. Brush the inside of the pie with egg wash, and sprinkle with just enough bread crumbs to lightly coat it.
6. Press two-thirds of the ground chicken mixture into the bottoms and sides of the pie, as you did with the pie dough (without rolling it out first), creating a meat shell or bowl inside the pie.
7. Arrange the browned squab or chicken thighs on the bottom of the pie, over the ground chicken mixture.
8. Add the mushrooms and shallots on top of the chicken thighs, smoothing it out.

Continued on page 44

7 ounces pancetta or ¾ cup chopped bacon

½ cup currants or raisins

1 teaspoon Northern Strong Spices (page 11)

1 teaspoon Old Valyrian Blend (page 11)

1x Strong Crust (page 10)

1/3 cup Madeira or Marsala wine

1/3 cup chicken broth

¾ teaspoon unflavored gelatin

PAIRS WELL WITH:

Kingswood Bramble Sauce (page 14), Northern Ale Preserves (page 14), or Hot Pie's Gravy (page 12)

> *Choked on his pigeon pie.*
>
> TYRION LANNISTER

9. In a small bowl, whisk together the wine, broth, and unflavored gelatin. Pour the liquid into the meat shell in the pie, just enough to cover the chicken thighs and half of the mushroom mixture. You may not have to use all the liquid.
10. Add the remaining ground chicken mixture on top, and spread it over the top, sealing it with the chicken mixture lining the sides. Make sure there are no holes for the liquid to escape; then sprinkle the top with more bread crumbs.
11. Brush some of the egg wash over the edges of the pie dough. Roll out the smaller portion of pie dough to a 12-inch circle, and drape it over the top of the pie. Seal the edges by pinching the sides and top dough together. Roll out the remaining dough to ¼-inch thickness, and use it to make any decorations you want to add. Brush the bottom of the decorations with egg wash to help them adhere to the top crust. An easy but effective decoration is to line the perimeter of the top of the pie with dough leaves.
12. Cut a hole in the center of the top crust to vent steam. Into the steam hole, insert a pie bird or a small piece of aluminum foil shaped into a funnel, to prevent the hole from closing. Generously brush the top of the pie with egg wash.
13. Transfer the springform pan to a rimmed baking sheet, and bake for 30 minutes. Reduce the oven temperature to 325°F, and continue to bake until the crust is a deep golden brown and an instant-read thermometer inserted into the center of the pie registers at least 165°F, about 60 to 90 minutes. Check on the pie periodically; you may need to drape the pie with aluminum foil to prevent the top crust from getting too browned or burnt.
14. Let the pie cool in the pan at room temperature for at least 2 hours before releasing it from the springform pan. Do not slice into the pie until it has cooled to room temperature, or the filling will not be set and will fall apart when sliced.
15. Serve slices with Kingswood Bramble Sauce, Northern Ale Preserves, or Hot Pie's Gravy.

YIELD: 4 SINGLE-SERVING PIES • PREP TIME: 45 MINUTES
COOKING TIME: 90 MINUTES • REST TIME: 20 MINUTES • DIFFICULTY: MODERATE

LAMPREY PIE

Lampreys were trapped by fishermen in the fresh and coastal waters of the Crownlands and brought to the kitchens of the Red Keep. There, the kitchen boys prepared them according to the cooks' own method. More meat flavored than fishy, the coveted eel flesh was simmered in an aromatic seasoned broth and baked into small flaky-crust pies. They were a known favorite of the Lannisters during the time of kings Joffrey and Tommen, and the demand kept trappers busy during the lampreys' spring and summer migration.

2 tablespoons unsalted butter, plus more for greasing

1 Flaky Crust (page 9)

4 garlic cloves, minced

4 anchovy filets

¼ teaspoon salt (plus more to taste)

1 sweet yellow onion, chopped

1 carrot, chopped

1 rib celery, chopped

1 bulb fennel, white parts only, thinly sliced

Black pepper

2 tablespoons olive tapenade or capers

1 teaspoon lemon zest

1 cup white wine

1 cup fish or mushroom stock

1 bay leaf

½ pound red potatoes, chopped

1 to 2 tablespoons granulated sugar

1 tablespoon Old Valyrian Blend (page 11)

1 teaspoon Westerosi Sweet Spice (page 11)

½ teaspoon saffron (optional)

¼ cup flat-leaf parsley, chopped

1 pound prepared eel or white fish, cut into 2-inch pieces

One 14-ounce package frozen puff pastry, thawed

1 egg, lightly beaten, for washing

1. Preheat the oven to 375°F. Generously grease four 12-ounce oven-safe ramekins with butter.
2. Roll out the Flaky Crust pie dough on a lightly floured surface to a rectangle about ⅛ inch thick. Cut out 4 discs roughly 6 inches wide, rerolling as necessary. Transfer these to the greased ramekins, and push them into the bottom and sides; leaving some overhang. Cover with plastic wrap, and place in the fridge until later.
3. Using a mortar and pestle, smash the garlic cloves, anchovy filets, and ¼ teaspoon salt into a paste. Set aside.
4. Melt the butter over medium heat in a Dutch oven over a heavy-bottomed soup pot. Add the onion, carrot, celery, and fennel, and season with salt and pepper to taste. Sauté, stirring occasionally, until the vegetables have softened slightly, about 5 minutes.
5. Add the garlic and anchovy paste. Cook, stirring occasionally, until the mixture is very fragrant, about 1 minute; then add the olive tapenade or capers, lemon zest and wine. Cook, stirring often, until the wine has reduced by nearly half, about 10 minutes.
6. Stir in the stock, bay leaf, potatoes, sugar, and spices. Bring to a simmer. Turn the heat to low, and simmer for 20 to 25 minutes until the broth has reduced. Stir in the parsley. Adjust seasoning to taste. Remove the bay leaf, and remove the pot from heat.
7. Season the eel or fish with salt and pepper, and divide it among the pastry-lined ramekins. Divide the sauce and the vegetables evenly among the ramekins. Set aside for now.
8. Roll out the puff pastry, and cut out four 5-inch discs to use as the tops of the pies. Transfer the tops to the ramekins, pinching the edges together to seal.
9. Cut a hole in the center of each pie to vent steam. Brush the tops of the pies with egg wash. Bake for 30 to 35 minutes until the crusts are golden brown and the filling is bubbling.
10. Let the pies cool for 15 to 20 minutes before serving. If you plan to remove the pies from the ramekins before serving, run a knife along the edges to loosen the pies enough to pop them out. Serve warm.

> “*Excellent lamprey pie. Were you slaving away in the kitchen all day?*”
>
> TYRION LANNISTER

V, V+*, GF • YIELD: 1 TO 2 SERVINGS • PREP TIME: 5 MINUTES
COOKING TIME: 15 MINUTES • REST TIME: 1 HOUR • DIFFICULTY: EASY

ICED MILK

Ice from the North, sawed in blocks from freshwater lakes and wrapped in sacking and hay, was sent by cart to the ice houses of the capital, great stone wells cut deep below the kitchens of King's Landing. The ice in these cold wells remained frozen even in the summer heat and was used to make sorbets, freeze cream desserts, and chill drinks such as iced milk.

2 cups milk

1 to 2 cinnamon sticks

1 to 2 cardamom pods, lightly crushed

Seeds of 1 vanilla pod (or use 1 teaspoon vanilla extract or paste)

1 tablespoon honey (or to taste)

Grated nutmeg or ground cinnamon, for serving (optional)

1. Add the milk, cinnamon sticks, cardamom pods, and vanilla seeds to a small pot on medium-high heat. Heat the milk, stirring, until just below boiling—don't let it boil. Remove from heat, cover, and let rest for about 10 minutes to allow the spices to infuse into the milk.
2. Mix a tablespoon of honey into the warm milk. Taste, and add more honey as desired.
3. You can opt to remove the spices or keep them in if you like stronger flavors. Transfer the milk to a sealable, heatproof storage container, such as a mason jar. Cover, and put in the refrigerator to cool for at least 1 hour. The infused milk can be stored in the refrigerator for up to 3 days.
4. When cooled, shake the milk to redistribute the sugars from the honey, which may have separated. Serve over ice, and garnish with an optional sprinkle of grated nutmeg or ground cinnamon.

> *Can I get you some iced milk and a nice bowl of raspberries, too?*
>
> TYRION LANNISTER

NOTE: *Bowl of Brown is a versatile stew that changes depending on what ingredients are available. Toss in whatever you have on hand: vegetables that are about to turn, leftover meat, grains such as barley or farro, legumes such as lentils or split peas, turnips or waxy potatoes, and so on.*

GF* • YIELD: 8 TO 10 SERVINGS • PREP TIME: 30 MINUTES
COOKING TIME: 3–8 HOURS (MOSTLY IDLE) • DIFFICULTY: MODERATE

BOWL OF BROWN

The smallfolk of Flea Bottom lived a precarious life in the slums of the capital. They thrived or starved on the whims of kings, living well in times of plenty or suffering when a poor harvest or war brought scarcity to their streets. The traders and artisans (the wheelwrights, blacksmiths, potters, weavers, and tanners) were fed by cooks from the pot-shops. These small kitchens sold bowls of steaming stew made from simple cuts of market meat and vegetables. Cheap bowls were little more than onions, cabbage, and gristle of dubious origin, but skilled cooks raised this basic broth into an art form. A good "bowl of brown," as they called it, was a fragrant, meat-filled fare of pork and sausage, seasoned and slow-cooked with mushrooms, root vegetables, and herbs. Cooks vied with one another for the best "brown," zealously guarding recipes that included ingredients such as prunes, dark beer, and spices.

2 pounds boneless pork shoulder, cut into 2-inch pieces

Salt

Black pepper

1 ounce dried wild or porcini mushrooms

1 tablespoon oil

1 pound smoked sausage, sliced

1 large yellow onion, chopped

4 garlic cloves, minced

2 ribs celery, chopped

2 large carrots, peeled and chopped

16 ounces fresh mushrooms, sliced

1 tablespoon apple cider vinegar

1 small green cabbage, cored and chopped

1 to 2 tablespoons Old Valyrian Blend (page 11)

1 teaspoon Northern Strong Spices (page 11) (optional)

2 bay leaves

2 tablespoons dried marjoram

One 16-ounce bottle dark beer

1½ cups beef broth

1 ham hock

15 prunes, pitted

3 tablespoons Worcestershire sauce

1. Season the pork liberally with salt and pepper. Set aside.
2. Soak the dried mushrooms in warm water for 10 minutes and then rinse them, removing any dirt. Soak them again in about 1 cup of water, and set them aside.
3. In a large skillet, heat the oil over medium-high heat. Working in batches so as not to overcrowd the meat, brown the pork pieces for 2 to 3 minutes. Set aside the browned pieces.
4. To the same skillet as the pork, add the sausage. Brown until a crust forms on the outside, about 2 to 3 minutes on each side. Remove the sausage, and set aside.
5. To the skillet, add the onions; sauté for 1 to 2 minutes. Add the minced garlic, and sauté for another minute. Add the celery, carrots, and fresh mushrooms, and continue to sauté for another 5 minutes until the mushrooms release their liquid. Add the apple cider vinegar and use a wooden spoon to scrape up the browned bits at the bottom of the pan.
6. Start adding the cabbage in handfuls at a time, adding more as it cooks down. If your skillet is too small, you can transfer everything to a large pot for this step. Stir in the spices, and season with salt and pepper. Continue to cook for 3 to 4 minutes until the vegetables are somewhat softened.
7. Transfer the veggies to a slow cooker. Add the bay leaves, marjoram, beer, broth, ham hock, prunes, Worcestershire sauce, dried mushrooms (along with the water they've been soaking in), and browned pork. Give everything a stir.
8. Cook in the slow cooker on low heat for 7 to 8 hours or on high heat for 3 to 4 hours. You also can cook it in a Dutch oven over very low heat on the stove for 2 to 3 hours; just be sure to check periodically to ensure that no burning occurs.
9. Taste, and adjust seasoning as desired. Serve hot with warm bread.

> *In Flea Bottom, we called them bowls of brown. We'd pretend that the meat in them was chicken. We knew it wasn't chicken.*
>
> GENDRY

V, V+, GF • YIELD: SERVES 2–4 • PREP TIME: 15 MINUTES • DIFFICULTY: EASY

POMEGRANATE JUICE

Pomegranates grew freely in the southern lands of Westeros and Essos. This fleshy red fruit with jewel-like carmine seeds was valued as a dessert. Most importantly, its juice was believed to be filled with health-giving and even aphrodisiac properties.

2 cups pomegranate arils (from 2 to 3 pomegranates)

2 cups water, divided

2 teaspoons lemon juice

Pinch of fine salt

2 tablespoons granulated sugar (or to taste)

1. Add the pomegranate arils, water, and lemon juice to a blender. Pulse for 10 seconds, just until the juice releases from the seeds.
2. Pour the juice through a fine mesh strainer. Using the back of a spoon, gently press down the seeds so that every drop of juice is released. You can also use cheesecloth to strain and squeeze the lingering juice.
3. Add the salt, sugar, and more water, to taste.
4. Store in a glass bottle or sealed jar in the refrigerator for up to 1 week. Serve chilled.

> *Are you hungry? Shall I have them bring you some cake or pomegranate juice?*
>
> TOMMEN BARATHEON

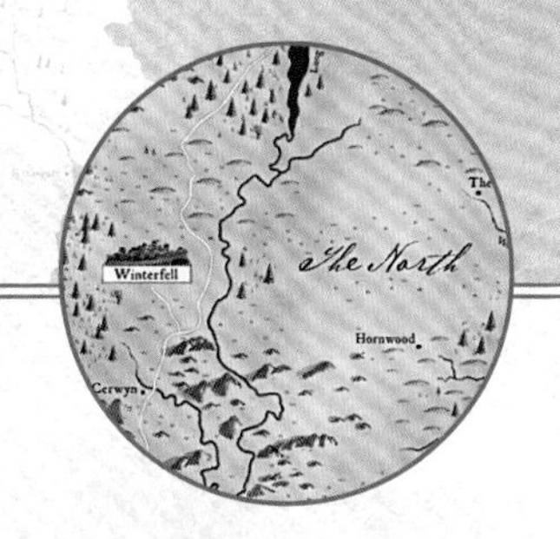

THE NORTH & BEYOND THE WALL

The food of the northernmost lands reflected the character of its people: rich but simple dishes of meat and mead, pies and bread for the nobles of Winterfell, sustaining stews for the men of the Night's Watch on the Wall, and drink rooted in myth for the Free Folk beyond.

GF* • YIELD: 6 SERVINGS • PREP TIME: 30 MINUTES
COOKING TIME: 3 HOURS • DIFFICULTY: MODERATE

HOBB'S VENISON STEW WITH ONIONS

When adequately provisioned, the soldiers of Castle Black ate simply but well. Life in the Night's Watch was hard, but competent Lord Commanders saw to it that the Brothers never went hungry. Deer were abundant in the Haunted Forest, and huntsmen on patrol brought venison to the kitchens. Skilled cooks turned basic stews into tasty meals for the Watchers on the Wall so that they had the strength to guard the realms of men.

2 pounds venison stew meat (or use beef chuck), trimmed and cut into 1-inch cubes

Salt

Black pepper

¼ cup all-purpose flour, plus 1 to 2 teaspoons for a slurry

6 strips bacon, chopped

1 tablespoon unsalted butter

2 large sweet yellow onions, roughly chopped

6 garlic cloves, minced

1 teaspoon dried thyme

1 teaspoon dried oregano

½ teaspoon dried rosemary

1 teaspoon Old Valyrian Blend (page 11)

2 tablespoons Worcestershire sauce

3 to 4 cups venison or beef stock, divided

1 to 2 cups brown ale or stout, divided

2 large carrots, roughly chopped

1 pound fingerling potatoes, halved lengthwise

1 pound pearl onions (peeled)

1. Pat the venison dry with a paper towel. Generously season the venison with salt and pepper, and toss the pieces in the flour until well coated.
2. Cook the bacon in a Dutch oven over medium-high heat until crisp. Set aside the bacon, but leave the fat in the pan.
3. In the bacon fat, brown the venison pieces on all sides. Be sure to work in batches, to avoid overcrowding the meat. Set aside the browned pieces.
4. Add the butter to the Dutch oven, and let it melt until it starts to bubble. Add the yellow onions, and cook for 2 to 3 minutes until fragrant; then add the garlic, herbs, and spices, and cook for another minute or two. Add the Worcestershire sauce, and scrape up any browned pieces remaining on the bottom of the pot.
5. To the Dutch oven, add back the browned venison and any leaked juices, along with the cooked bacon, 3 cups of the stock, and 1 cup of the ale. Cover the pot with a lid, and simmer over low heat for 1 hour.
6. Add the carrots and potatoes to the pot, and simmer on low heat for 1 more hour. Then add the pearl onions, and simmer for another 20 minutes until the broth has reduced and the vegetables and venison are tender. Add more stock or ale as needed.
7. Whisk together 1 to 2 teaspoons of flour with 1 tablespoon water, and stir it into the stew. Continue to simmer for 5 to 10 minutes until the broth thickens to a gravy-like consistency. Taste, and adjust seasoning.
8. Serve hot in a hollow bread bowl or with warm buttered bread on the side.

> *Castle Black is nice enough. They keep a fire burning in the long hall day and night. And Hobb makes venison stew with onions. Very tasty. Sometimes one of the brothers will sing.*
>
> SAMWELL TARLY

YIELD: 8 TO 10 SERVINGS • PREP TIME: 45 MINUTES
COOKING TIME: 2 HOURS • DIFFICULTY: MODERATE

RAT COOK'S PIE

This chicken and bacon pie was named for the mythical Rat Cook of the Nightfort, a vast abandoned castle on the Wall. Legend told of a king's visit in the days when the fort was manned. The cook, angry with his king for some unknown slight, killed the king's son and served him to the king in a pie. So cruelly had the cook contravened the laws of hospitality that, in their fury, the gods turned him into a huge white rat. As further punishment, they made him eternally ravenous and decreed that he could eat only his own young. The pie was a macabre celebration of the legend and famed for its fine flavor.

6 to 8 boneless, skinless chicken thighs, cut into 2-inch pieces

1 teaspoon Northern Strong Spices (page 11)

Salt

Black pepper

3 tablespoons flour

6 strips thick-cut bacon

1 large yellow onion, chopped

4 garlic cloves, minced

16 ounces baby bella mushrooms, sliced

1 large carrot, chopped

2 teaspoons Old Valyrian Blend (page 11)

1 cup chicken broth

1 cup dark red wine

2 bay leaves

½ cup heavy cream

1 cup Alpine cheese (such as Gruyère, Beaufort, or Emmental), grated

1 Flaky Crust (page 9)

1 egg, lightly beaten, for washing

1. Season the chicken with spices and salt and pepper. Coat the pieces in the flour. Set aside.
2. In a large skillet, cook the bacon until crispy. When cool enough, remove the bacon with a slotted spoon. Crumble the bacon, and set it aside, but keep the bacon fat hot in the pan.
3. In batches, brown the chicken pieces in the bacon fat for 2 to 3 minutes on each side. Set aside the browned pieces.
4. Add the chopped yellow onion to the pan, and sauté for 2 to 3 minutes until translucent. Add the garlic, and cook for another minute until fragrant. Add the mushrooms and carrot; season with Old Valyrian Blend, salt, and pepper; and cook for 7 to 8 minutes, stirring occasionally, until the mushrooms brown and the carrots soften.
5. Add the broth, wine, and bay leaves, and then return the chicken and bacon to the skillet. Adjust the seasoning as desired, and stir. Bring to a simmer; then reduce heat to medium-low, and cook for 20 minutes or until thickened. Stir in the cream, and continue to simmer for another minute or two. Add half of the cheese, and stir until the cheese has melted into the sauce, about 1 to 2 minutes. Set aside the filling to cool to almost room temperature.
6. Preheat the oven to 400°F. Grease a 9- or 10-inch cast-iron skillet. It can be the same one you used to cook the filling—just transfer the filling to a bowl temporarily and clean the skillet. A 10-inch deep-dish pie plate or an 8-inch springform pan can also be used.

Continued on page 58

When the king was visiting the Nightfort, the cook killed the king's son, cooked him into a big pie with onions, carrots, mushrooms, and bacon. That night he served the pie to the king. He liked the taste of his son so much, he asked for a second slice. The gods turned the cook into a giant white rat who could only eat his own young. He's been roaming the Nightfort ever since, devouring his own babies. But no matter what he does, he's always hungry.

BRAN ”

7. Roll out the pie dough 2 to 4 inches larger than the size of your cooking vessel, and line it by pressing the dough into the bottom and sides. Roll out a separate piece of dough slightly larger than the diameter of your cooking vessel to use as the top crust.
8. Remove the bay leaves, and transfer the filling to your prepared pie dish. Sprinkle the remaining cheese over the top of the filling. Brush the edges with egg wash, and cover with the top crust, pinching the sides to seal. Crimp the edges or apply decor as you like. Brush the crust with more egg wash, and cut holes or slits in the top crust to vent steam.
9. Bake on the lower rack for 30 to 35 minutes until the crust is golden brown and the inside is bubbling. You may need to tent the pie with aluminum foil for the last 5 to 10 minutes to prevent burning, depending on your oven. Cool slightly before serving.

GF • YIELD: 4 SERVINGS • PREP TIME: 15 MINUTES
COOKING TIME: 30 MINUTES • DIFFICULTY: EASY

PORK CHOPS AND APPLES

Herbed and seasoned pork chops were considered the height of epicurean delight in the North. The flavorful salted cuts sat well with the soft, sweetened apples in a dish that was loved by the rich and revered by the poor.

- 4 thick bone-in pork chops
- 2 teaspoons fine salt (or to taste)
- 1½ teaspoons Old Valyrian Blend (page 11)
- 1½ teaspoons Northern Strong Spices (page 11)
- ⅓ cup brown sugar
- ½ teaspoon cinnamon
- ¼ teaspoon nutmeg
- 1 teaspoon spicy brown mustard
- 1 teaspoon apple cider vinegar
- ¼ cup unsalted butter, divided
- 2 yellow onions, chopped
- 1 tablespoon chopped fresh sage leaves
- 2 to 3 sprigs fresh thyme
- 2 Honeycrisp apples, peeled, cored, and sliced

PAIRS WELL WITH:
Hot Pie's Gravy (page 12)

1. Pat the pork chops dry, and season on both sides with the salt, Old Valyrian Blend, and Northern Strong Spices. Let the pork rest and absorb the spices for 30 minutes.
2. In a small bowl, mix together the brown sugar, cinnamon, nutmeg, mustard, vinegar, and 2 tablespoons water. Set aside
3. In a large skillet (ideally, cast iron), melt 2 tablespoons butter over medium heat. Add the pork chops, and cook for 4 to 5 minutes on each side until they are nicely browned and the internal temperature reaches 145°F. You may need to do this in batches, depending on the size of your skillet; don't overcrowd the pan, or the meat won't brown properly.
4. Remove the pork chops from the skillet, and set aside. In the same skillet over medium heat, melt 1 tablespoon butter. Add the onions, sage, and thyme, and sauté for 4 to 5 minutes until the onions have softened and browned slightly. Add the apples and brown sugar mixture, and cook, stirring occasionally, until the apples are tender but not mushy, about 15 to 18 minutes. You may need to occasionally add a tablespoon of water or the drippings from the pork chops if the sauce is reducing too much before the apples are tender.
5. Remove the thyme sprigs and add the pork chops, along with any juices, back into the pan. Cook for another minute or two, just to heat the pork chops. Serve the chops with the apples, onions, and sauce.

"*Prince Porkchop. Where is he?*"

PYP

V, GF • YIELD: 8 SERVINGS • PREP TIME: 30 MINUTES
COOKING TIME: 1 HOUR • DIFFICULTY: EASY

ARMORED TURNIPS

The turnip was a staple food for the people of the North and their animals. Creative cooks of Winterfell raised this simple root to gourmet status with a dish of sliced turnip, layered into a gratin like the scales on a dragon or the stitched rondels of leather armor.

The North sent turnips to the kingdoms of Westeros by cart, but it was by no means their only export. Many smallfolk paid coppers to the drivers or bartered a ride to the capital. Children were even known to stow away under the vegetables, but it was a long, rough ride, and few remained hidden all the way.

1 teaspoon Northern Strong Spices (page 11)

1 to 2 teaspoons salt (or to taste)

½ cup grated Parmesan cheese, divided

6 to 8 medium turnips, peeled, trimmed, and sliced ¼ inch thick

¼ cup unsalted butter, melted, plus more for greasing dish

2 garlic cloves, minced, divided

1 cup grated Alpine cheese (such as Gruyère or Emmental)

1 cup grated sharp white cheddar or Jarlsberg cheese

1 cup milk or half-and-half

Chopped parsley, for serving (optional)

1. Preheat the oven to 375°F. Grease a 9-by-13-inch casserole dish or a 3- quart baking dish with butter.
2. In a small bowl, stir together the spices and salt.
3. Sprinkle a quarter of the Parmesan cheese on the bottom of the baking dish, and then arrange the turnips with their edges overlapping into a single layer in the dish.
4. Sprinkle on a third of the butter, then a third of the spices and garlic, and finally a third of the Parmesan and grated cheeses.
5. Repeat with the remaining turnips, butter, and spices. On the final layer, hold off on the cheeses; you will add them later.
6. After layering, pour the milk or half-and-half over everything.
7. Cover the dish with aluminum foil, and bake for 40 to 50 minutes. Remove the foil, and blot away any excess grease on the top. The turnips should be fork tender. Add the final layer of Parmesan and grated cheeses.
8. Broil at 500°F for 4 to 6 minutes until the cheese is bubbly and lightly browned. Garnish with chopped parsley, if desired.
9. Allow to cool for 5 to 10 minutes before serving.

GF* • YIELD: 6 SERVINGS • PREP TIME: 30 MINUTES
COOKING TIME: 1 HOUR • DIFFICULTY: EASY

RAMSEY SNOW'S PORK SAUSAGE

The charcutiers, or flesh cooks, of Winterfell made fine pork sausages according to their own special recipes. Served simply with condiments and with bread, alongside potatoes, or on a bed of caramelized onions and gravy, they were a northern speciality.

1 to 2 tablespoons oil

6 to 8 pork bratwursts (or similar sausages)

2 tablespoons unsalted butter

4 large yellow onions, sliced

1 tablespoon brown sugar

1 tablespoon Old Valyrian Blend (page 11)

2 teaspoons fresh thyme leaves

1 teaspoon dried marjoram

½ teaspoon dried tarragon

½ teaspoon juniper berries, lightly crushed (optional)

¼ teaspoon Northern Strong Spices (page 11)

Salt

Black pepper

⅔ cup lager beer

⅔ cup apple cider

⅔ cup chicken broth

1 teaspoon potato or corn starch

PAIRS WELL WITH:

A grainy mustard or Northern Ale Preserves (page 14)

1. Preheat the oven to 350°F.
2. Heat the oil in a Dutch oven over medium-high heat. Brown the sausages, rotating them, until caramelized on all sides. Transfer the sausages to a plate, and set aside.
3. Reduce heat to medium-low. In the same Dutch oven, melt the butter. Add the onions, brown sugar, Old Valyrian Blend, herbs, juniper berries, Northern Strong Spices, and salt and pepper to taste; stir to combine. Sauté on medium-low heat for 25 to 30 minutes, stirring every 5 to 6 minutes, until the onions are caramelized.
4. Add the cooked sausages back, along with the beer, cider, and broth. In a small bowl, whisk together the potato or corn starch and 1 tablespoon of water; then stir the slurry into the liquid in the pot.
5. Bring to a simmer over high heat for 4 to 5 minutes until reduced slightly. Transfer to the oven, and cook uncovered for 18 to 20 minutes until the sausages are cooked through and the gravy has thickened. Taste, and adjust seasoning as desired.
6. Serve individual sausages on a bed of onions and gravy with Northern Ale Preserves or mustard applied along the length of the sausage.

V • YIELD: 8 SERVINGS • PREP TIME: 30 MINUTES
COOKING TIME: 30 MINUTES • DIFFICULTY: EASY

WINTERFELL BREAD PUDDING

Warm puddings were a staple of northern cuisine, and the simplest and best were made from bread. Thrifty cooks used leftover crusts and loaf ends, with milk, eggs, and cream from the dairy to bake a comforting sweet worthy of noble houses.

3 eggs, lightly beaten

1½ cups whole milk

1 cup heavy cream

½ cup brown sugar

1 tablespoon Westerosi Sweet Spice (page 11)

1 teaspoon vanilla extract

½ cup unsalted butter, melted and cooled, divided

8 cups white bread, slightly stale, cut into 1-inch cubes

1 cup currants, raisins, or fresh cranberries

Confectioner's sugar, for dusting

Whipped cream or ice cream, for serving (optional)

1. Preheat the oven to 350°F. Grease a 9-by-9-inch baking dish with butter.
2. In a large mixing bowl, whisk together the eggs, milk, cream, sugar, spices, and vanilla, along with half (4 tablespoons) of the butter.
3. Add the bread and currants, raisins, or cranberries to the mixing bowl, and stir to combine. Allow the bread to soak in the mixture for about 5 minutes.
4. Transfer the bread mixture to the prepared baking dish, and spread it out evenly. As evenly as possible, drizzle another 2 tablespoons of the butter over the top.
5. Bake for 20 to 25 minutes until the top is golden brown and the inside is set.
6. Brush the top with the remaining 2 tablespoons of butter, and let set for 5 minutes.
7. Dust the top with confectioner's sugar, and let cool for a few more minutes. Serve warm with whipped cream, ice cream, or Kingswood Bramble Sauce, if desired.

PAIRS WELL WITH:

Kingswood Bramble Sauce (page 14)

"*My mother, fat? She never let me have my pudding until I'd finished all my proper food.*"

SANSA STARK

MANCE RAYDER'S PROPER NORTHERN DRINK

The Free Folk drank fermented milk instead of ale or wine. This ancient alcoholic drink was traditionally made from goat's milk, with sweeteners and spices to taste. The tribes stored the drink in skin bags, chilling it with snow to drink.

1 cup plain kefir

1 cup milk

½ cup vodka (optional)

3 tablespoons dark maple syrup (or to taste)

1 teaspoon cinnamon

¼ teaspoon ground ginger

Pinch of salt

¾ cup ice

1. Add all ingredients to a blender.
2. Blend until fully incorporated.
3. Pour into 2 glasses, and serve.

> *It's a proper northern drink, Jon Snow.*
>
> MANCE RAYDER

WALNUT PIE

Walnuts were grown in the orchards of the south and harvested in the fall. Many thousands of sacks were transported to the North, where the cold, dry climate provided perfect conditions for storage through winter and spring. Sweet pies were the preferred winter dish, made with toasted walnuts, maple syrup, and a soft butter crust.

2½ cups walnuts, roughly chopped

½ Sweet Crust (page 10)

2 large eggs, lightly beaten

1 cup dark or very dark maple syrup (or use ¾ cup honey mixed with ¼ cup molasses)

1 teaspoon vanilla extract

2 tablespoons unsalted butter, melted, plus more for greasing

2 tablespoons all-purpose flour

½ teaspoon fine salt

1 teaspoon Westerosi Sweet Spice (page 11)

1. Preheat the oven to 400°F. Line a rimmed baking sheet with parchment paper.
2. Scatter the walnuts on the parchment-lined baking sheet, spreading them out evenly, and toast in the oven for about 5 to 7 minutes or until walnuts start to become fragrant. Keep an eye on them, making sure they don't burn. Transfer the walnuts to a heatproof bowl or other heatproof container, and set them aside to cool.
3. Reduce the oven heat to 375°F.
4. Grease a 9-inch pie or tart tin with butter. On a lightly floured surface, roll out the Sweet Crust dough to an approximately 11-inch circle; then transfer it to the pie tin, and press it into the bottom and sides of the tin, cutting off any excess. If you'd like, use any excess dough to create decorative leaves or other shapes. Set aside.
5. In a large mixing bowl, whisk together the eggs, maple syrup, vanilla extract, and melted butter. While continuing to whisk, sprinkle in the flour, salt, and spices. Whisk until smooth.
6. Scatter the cooled walnuts into the prepared pie or tart shell. Pour the maple syrup mixture over the walnuts. Arrange the decorative pie pieces on top, if using.
7. Place the pie in the oven on the middle rack. Place a cookie sheet on the rack directly below the pie, to catch any filling that might spill over when heated.
8. Bake for 40 to 45 minutes. About halfway through baking, drape a sheet of aluminum foil over the pie to prevent the edges from burning.
9. Remove the pie from the oven, and let it cool completely before serving.

> *Eleven men. Most of them already drunk. No guards posted. They don't seem to have a care in the world. We'll carve them up like walnut pie.*
>
> LOCKE

GF • YIELD: 8 TO 10 SERVINGS • PREP TIME: 40 MINUTES
COOKING TIME: 3 HOURS • DIFFICULTY: MODERATE

MEAT AND MEAD

The Westerosi vow of "Meat and Mead," given by Sansa Stark to Brienne of Tarth in return for her pledge of protection to the future Queen of the North, was written in the annals and taken to heart by many Northern cooks. The dish they made to honor their queen varied according to season and taste, but this rich pork and fruit stew with fragrant mead sauce was made on her name day to celebrate Northern independence, as granted by Bran I the Broken. Many also made the stew to celebrate Queen Sansa's savior, Brienne of Tarth, who became Lord Commander of the King's Guard.

One 4- to 5-pound bone-in pork shoulder

3 to 4 tablespoons Old Valyrian Blend (page 11), divided

1 tablespoon fine salt, divided (or to taste)

Black pepper

2 to 3 sprigs fresh thyme

1 sprig fresh rosemary

1 sprigs fresh sage

2 sprigs fresh tarragon

2 bay leaves

2 tablespoons oil, plus more as needed

2 onions, roughly chopped

6 garlic cloves, minced

1 bulb fennel, sliced

1 tablespoon apple cider vinegar

2 cups mead

2 to 3 cups chicken broth

4 to 5 pears, cored and quartered

½ cup heavy cream

1 to 2 tablespoons honey

PAIRS WELL WITH:

Mashed potatoes or turnips or warm bread (Refer to "Bread and Salt" recipe on page 93), for serving (optional)

1. Preheat the oven to 325°F.
2. Cut the pork into 2 to 3 large pieces of roughly the same size, cutting around the bone. Pat the pork dry with paper towels, and season it all over with half the Old Valyrian Blend, 2 to 3 teaspoons salt, and black pepper to taste. Set it aside.
3. Use kitchen twine to tie together the thyme, rosemary, sage, tarragon, and bay leaves. Set aside.
4. Heat the oil in a large Dutch oven over medium-high heat. When the oil is hot, arrange the pork in a single layer. Depending on the size of the Dutch oven and the shape of the pork pieces, you may need to do this in batches, to prevent crowding. Sear for 4 to 5 minutes on all sides until the pork is deeply browned. Remove the pork from the pot, and set aside.
5. Add the onions to the Dutch oven, and sauté over medium-high heat for 2 to 3 minutes. Add the minced garlic, fennel, and remaining Old Valyrian Blend, and sauté for another 4 to 5 minutes until softened somewhat. Add the vinegar, and scrape up any remaining browned bits on the bottom of the Dutch oven with a wooden spoon.
6. Transfer the browned pork back to the Dutch oven, toss in the herb bundle, and pour the mead and chicken broth over the top. You need just enough liquid to cover the meat, so you may need slightly more or slightly less than 4 cups of liquid. Bring to a simmer, cover, and place in the oven for 90 minutes. Add the pears to the pot, and then continue to cook until the meat is fork tender and shreddable and the pears are soft, about 30 to 45 minutes more.

Continued on page 72

7. Remove the pork and pears from the Dutch oven. Set the pot on the stove, and reduce the sauce by simmering it over medium-high heat for 10 to 15 minutes while the pork rests. Remove from heat, and stir the cream and honey into the broth. Taste the broth, and adjust the seasoning to taste.
8. Slice or shred the pork, and serve with the pears and broth. Serve over mashed potatoes or turnips or in a bread bowl or trencher, and garnish with fresh thyme sprigs, if desired.

“*I vow that you should always have a place at my hearth . . .*

SANSA STARK”

YIELD: 2 TO 4 SERVINGS • PREP TIME: 15 MINUTES
COOKING TIME: 30 MINUTES • DIFFICULTY: EASY

BREAKFAST OF THE NORTH

Breakfast was a traveler's most important meal. But for many travelers, eggs, bacon, and blood sausage, accompanied by soft bread fried to a perfect crisp in the fats and washed down with beer, was a fantasy. Most would be lucky to eat a hard crust dipped in pine needle tea.

3 to 5 tablespoons unsalted butter, divided (or as needed)

4 ounces black pudding, sliced (or use another blood sausage)

4 slices loin or back bacon (or use thick-cut bacon)

4 large eggs

4 thick slices of bread

Dark beer, such as stout or porter, for serving (optional)

PAIRS WELL WITH:

Northern Ale Preserves (page 14)

1. Melt 1 tablespoon of butter in a large nonstick skillet over medium-high heat. When the skillet is hot, place the black pudding and bacon rashers on the skillet at the same time; cook, turning once, until browned and heated through, about 5 to 6 minutes or 2 to 3 minutes per side. If your skillet is too small, brown the sausage first and then cook the bacon. Remove the sausage and bacon, and set aside; keep the fat in the pan.
2. Fry the bread in the fat about 2 to 3 minutes per side until crisp and golden, flipping and adding 1 to 2 tablespoons of butter as needed. Remove, and set aside.
3. Wipe down the skillet; then melt a tablespoon of butter over medium heat. Crack the eggs in batches of 2 to 4 in the skillet; fry, covered, until the whites are set but the yolks are still runny, about 3 minutes. Add more butter as needed to prevent sticking.
4. Add to each serving plate 1 to 2 slices of bread, 1 to 2 eggs, 1 to 2 rashers, and 1 to 2 sausages. Serve with Northern Ale Preserves and dark beer to wash it down.

"*Eat something that isn't moss. I want an egg. How do you like 'em? Boiled? Fried up with some butter?*"

MEERA REED

V, GF • YIELD: 4 TO 6 SERVINGS • PREP TIME: 10 MINUTES
COOKING TIME: 15 MINUTES • DIFFICULTY: EASY

GIANT'S MILK

The legendary Tormund Giantsbane, warrior of the Free Folk, was said to have gotten his mighty strength and size from giant's milk. Whether true or just an old fireside story, "giant's milk," made with egg yolk and spiced tea, was renowned for lending potency, courage, and vigour to the drinker.

1 spiced tea bag (such as chai, cinnamon, or orange spice)

1 cup hot water

2 cups whole milk

4 egg yolks, lightly beaten

One 12-ounce can sweetened condensed milk, divided (or to taste)

1 teaspoon vanilla extract

1 to 2 drops walnut bitters (optional)

½ cup rum or brandy (optional)

1. Add the tea bag to the hot water, and let it steep. Set aside until needed.
2. Whisk together the whole milk and egg yolks in the top of a double boiler over simmering water, stirring constantly, until the mixture is thick enough to coat the back of a spoon. You can do this in a saucepan over low heat, but you must be more careful not to overcook the mixture, which will cause it to separate and become lumpy.
3. Transfer the yolk mixture to a blender. Add half the sweetened condensed milk, the extracts, and half the brewed tea, and blend until combined, about 30 seconds. If you want it to be thinner, add more of the tea until it reaches your desired consistency. If you want it to be sweeter, add more sweetened condensed milk until it's sweet enough.
4. If serving warm, serve it immediately. If serving chilled, pour the milk mixture into glass bottles or mason jars, and chill for at least 2 hours (or overnight) before serving.
5. If adding rum or brandy, add it to the individual serving glasses, and stir it in before serving.

> *When she woke up, you know what she did? Suckled me at her teat for three months. Thought I was her baby. That's how I got so strong. Giant's milk.*
>
> TORMUND GIANTSBANE

V*, V+* GF • YIELD: SERVES 4 • PREP TIME: 20 MINUTES
COOKING TIME: 90 MINUTES • DIFFICULTY: MODERATE

ROASTED POTATOES

Russet potatoes, grown and harvested throughout much of Westeros, were a revered vegetable in the North. Stocks laid in for long winters helped many families survive the cold. The potatoes were often served boiled, crushed, or sautéed. Northern connoisseurs, however, preferred them roasted in bacon fat, with garlic, herbs, and salt.

1 teaspoon baking soda

1 tablespoon fine salt

4 pounds russet potatoes, scrubbed and cut into 2-inch chunks (peeling optional)

½ cup bacon fat (or use another animal fat or a neutral oil)

6 garlic cloves, minced

2 tablespoons fresh rosemary, leaves only, finely chopped

2 tablespoons fresh thyme, leaves only, finely chopped

Coarse salt

Ground black pepper

2 to 3 tablespoons chopped fresh chives

1. Preheat the oven to 425°F. Line a large rimmed baking sheet with parchment paper.
2. In a large pot, whisk the baking soda and salt into approximately 7 to 8 cups water. Bring the water to a boil over medium-high heat; then reduce to a simmer. Add the potatoes, and simmer until the potatoes are soft enough to be pierced with a fork with a little resistance, about 10 to 12 minutes.
3. Meanwhile, melt the bacon fat in a small saucepan over medium-low heat. Cook the garlic, rosemary, and thyme in the bacon fat for 3 to 4 minutes, stirring frequently to prevent the garlic from sinking and burning. Use a slotted spoon to remove the herbs and garlic, and set them aside. Reserve the bacon fat in the pan.
4. Drain the potatoes, and let them rest in the pot for 2 minutes; then add the melted fat from the pan. Season to taste with coarse salt and pepper. Stir the potatoes until a thick, starchy paste forms around them.
5. Transfer the potatoes to the baking sheet, and spread them out evenly. Roast the potatoes in the preheated oven for 20 to 25 minutes.
6. Use a spatula to flip the potatoes. Continue roasting until the potatoes are golden brown and crisp all over, about 25 to 30 minutes longer.
7. Transfer the potatoes to a large mixing bowl. Add the sautéed garlic and herbs, the fresh chives, and additional coarse salt and pepper to taste. Toss to coat. Serve immediately.

> *Food's worth more than gold. Noble ladies sell their diamonds for a sack of potatoes.*
>
> BRONN

HOT SPICED CIDER

Cider from the presses of smallholdings and farms was taken warm in winter, simmered in a pot with spices and served steaming to alleviate the cold. It was a favorite of Winterfell feasts, served to children without alcohol, and much favored by the men of the Night's Watch. Many chose the hot, spiced drink over mulled wine, claiming wine made them drowsy on cold night watches on the Wall.

4 cups apple cider or unfiltered apple juice

4 cinnamon sticks

4 whole cloves

2 whole allspice berries

2 whole black peppercorns

4 strips orange peel, with no pith

4 to 8 ounces spiced rum or apple brandy (optional)

1. Add all ingredients except the rum or apple brandy to a small saucepan. Bring to a low simmer over medium-low heat, but do not boil. Simmer for 25 to 30 minutes
2. Remove the whole spices with a slotted spoon or a fine mesh strainer.
3. Add 1 to 2 ounces rum or apple brandy to 4 mugs. Top up each with the hot cider.
4. Garnish with cinnamon sticks, and serve.

THE RIVERLANDS & THE VALE OF ARRYN

The Riverlands and the Vale of Arryn lie across the center of the long continent of Westeros. To the west, the Riverlands' temperate climate and fertile river basins provided ample food for its people. To the east, the green valleys of the mountainous Vale offered a bounty of crops and game. Both regions had a simple culinary tradition based on seasonal foods that included breads, pies, and tarts.

YIELD: 6 TO 8 SERVINGS • PREP TIME: 40 MINUTES
COOKING TIME: 3 HOURS • DIFFICULTY: MODERATE

MUTTON STEW

Stew sustained armies and won battles, or so the cooks at Harrenhal believed. Soldiers were fed with steaming bowls of meat, root vegetables, and dark ale, seasoned with the best herbs the field kitchen boys could find.

2 pounds mutton or lamb shoulder, cut into 1- to 2-inch pieces

2 teaspoons Northern Strong Spices (page 11)

2 teaspoons ground cumin

1 to 2 teaspoons salt (or to taste)

½ teaspoon pepper (or to taste)

2 bay leaves

2 to 3 sprigs fresh rosemary

2 large leeks, with the white and light green parts sliced (reserve 1 sheet of the dark green outer leaf)

1 tablespoon oil

2 tablespoons unsalted butter, divided

6 garlic cloves, minced

3 carrots, roughly chopped

2 ribs celery, finely chopped

2 tablespoons Old Valyrian Blend (page 11)

2 cups red wine, divided

¼ cup all-purpose flour

4 cups beef broth

2 to 3 turnips, peeled and cut into 1-inch pieces

¼ cup chopped fresh mint, parsley, or cilantro, plus more for garnish

¾ cup pearl barley

PAIRS WELL WITH:

Bread and Salt (page 93) or Brown Bread (page 87)

1. Season the lamb with Northern Strong Spices, cumin, salt, and pepper.
2. Wrap the bay leaves and rosemary sprigs in the dark green leek leaf, and secure it with kitchen twine.
3. In a large Dutch oven or thick-bottomed soup pot, heat 1 tablespoon oil over medium-high heat, and brown the lamb pieces in small batches. Remove the browned lamb pieces, and set aside. Add more oil as needed.
4. In the same pot, melt 1 tablespoon of the butter. Add the sliced leeks, and sauté for 3 to 4 minutes until tender; then add the garlic, carrots, celery, and Old Valyrian Blend, and sauté for another 5 to 6 minutes until the carrots have softened. Remove the veggies from the pot, and set aside.
5. Deglaze the pot with a tablespoon or two of the wine, scraping any remaining brown bits from the bottom.
6. In the same pot, melt the remaining tablespoon of butter, and whisk in the flour. Cook for 1 minute, whisking frequently to prevent burning. Reduce heat to medium-low. Add the remaining wine a small amount at a time, mixing until smooth after each addition. When the wine has been fully incorporated, start adding the broth. The mixture will seem a little thick at first: Continue to whisk in the broth a little at a time until smooth.
7. Add the lamb and veggies back to the pot, along with the herb parcel you made earlier. Simmer, partially covered, on low heat for 60 to 80 minutes or until the lamb is tender.
8. Add the turnips, chopped fresh herbs, and barley. Simmer on low heat, covered, for another 35 to 45 minutes or until the turnips and barley are softened and the lamb is fork tender. Remove and discard the herb parcel. Taste, and adjust seasonings as desired; add more broth as needed.
9. Serve hot in a hollow bread bowl or with warm buttered bread on the side. Garnish with chopped herbs, if desired.

> “*Don't like mutton.*”
>
> TYWIN LANNISTER

HOT PIE'S SOUR CHERRY TARTS

Westerosi sour cherries, in season from late spring, were gathered from the trees by the basket and sold by roadside peddlers. Clever cooks turned them into sweet-crust tarts. The sour fruits were perfectly complemented by an egg-and-butter wash and a crushed almond topping that turned golden when baked.

4 cups fresh or frozen sour cherries, pitted

1 teaspoon orange zest

2 tablespoons lemon juice

⅔ cup dark brown sugar (or to taste)

¼ cup potato or corn starch

¾ cup water or tart cherry juice, divided

1 teaspoon vanilla extract

¼ teaspoon almond extract (optional)

¼ teaspoon fine salt

2 teaspoons Westerosi Sweet Spice (page 11), divided

1 Flaky Crust (page 9)

2 tablespoons bread crumbs

3 tablespoons cold unsalted butter, cubed, divided

1 egg, lightly beaten, for washing

¼ cup raw sugar

⅓ cup sliced almonds

1. Preheat the oven to 400°F. Line a large rimmed cookie sheet with parchment paper.
2. In a medium mixing bowl, combine the cherries with the lemon juice and brown sugar. Let sit for 10 to 15 minutes.
3. In a small bowl, whisk together the potato starch and 4 tablespoons of the water or juice to create a slurry.
4. To a medium saucepan over medium heat, add the cherries, orange zest, and any liquid in the bowl, the slurry, the vanilla and almond extracts, the salt, 1 teaspoon of the Westerosi Sweet Spice, and the remaining water or juice. Cook, stirring frequently, until the liquid thickens to a gooey, syrup-like consistency. Taste, and adjust the sweetness as desired. Set aside, and let cool for 5 to 10 minutes.
5. Roll out one of the pie crusts into a roughly circular shape about ¼ inch thick. Place the rolled dough on one side of a parchment-lined baking sheet. Sprinkle 1 tablespoon bread crumbs around the center of the crust.
6. Spoon half the cherries into the center, leaving a 2-inch border of crust. Top with half the cubed butter. Fold the crust over the cherry filling, sealing the overlapping edges with egg wash. Brush the crust with the beaten egg wash, making sure to get in between the folds so that they will seal when baked.
7. In a small bowl, mix together the raw sugar and remaining Westerosi Sweet Spice. If you like, hammer the almonds a few times with a mallet, to break them up a little. Sprinkle the crust of the tarts with half the crushed almonds and half the spiced sugar mixture.
8. Repeat the process to create another tart.
9. Place both tarts in the freezer for 10 minutes, to help them hold their shape when baked.
10. Bake the tarts in the middle rack of the oven until the crusts are golden and the insides are gently bubbling, about 30 to 35 minutes.

NOTE: *If sour cherries are not in season, you can use two 14- to 16-ounce cans of sour or tart cherries in water. Drain the cherries, but reserve the liquid. Add the liquid but not the cherries to the saucepan in step 4. When the liquid thickens to a gooey, syrup-like consistency, let it cool for 5 to 10 minutes; then gently fold in the cherries. Continue with the rest of the recipe as described.*

> *"You need sour cherries to make it right. And the secret is you dry the stones, and then you break them with a mallet. That's where the real flavor is. You crush 'em up real fine. And then when you're finished, you sprinkle them over the pie crust."*
>
> HOT PIE

V, V+* • YIELD: 1 LOAF • PREP TIME: 30 MINUTES • COOKING TIME: 40 MINUTES
REST TIME: 30 MINUTES • DIFFICULTY: MODERATE

BROWN BREAD

Bread made with butter and molasses was a Riverlands speciality. The hearty loaves, baked in a heavy iron pot, were eaten buttered or plain, dunked in soups and stews, or dipped in oil and salt.

- 2 cups whole-wheat flour
- 2 cups all-purpose flour
- 3 tablespoons wheat germ
- 2 teaspoons baking powder
- 1½ teaspoons baking soda
- 1 teaspoon fine salt
- 1½ tablespoons butter, chilled and cubed
- 1½ cups buttermilk (or more as needed)
- 2 tablespoons molasses

1. Preheat the oven to 450°F. Line a medium cast-iron skillet or a Dutch oven with parchment paper.
2. To a large mixing bowl, add the flours, wheat germ, baking powder, baking soda, and salt. Whisk to mix until well combined.
3. With clean fingers, rub in the butter until it resembles coarse crumbs.
4. Pour in most of the buttermilk and the molasses, and stir them into the dry ingredients. If the mixture still seems dry, stir in the rest of the buttermilk. If it is still dry, add a tablespoon or two more of the buttermilk until it's no longer crumbly.
5. Turn out the dough onto a lightly floured surface. Gently knead the dough a few times just to bring it together; don't overknead.
6. Shape the dough into a ball roughly 8 inches in diameter, and place the dough into the lined skillet or Dutch oven. Use a sharp knife to slash a cross into the top of the dough.
7. Place in the oven, and bake for 10 minutes; then reduce the temperature to 375°F, and bake for another 35 to 40 minutes until the internal temperature is 200°F. The bread should be risen and browned and should sound hollow when tapped on the bottom.
8. Transfer the bread to a cooling rack, and let it cool for at least 30 minutes before slicing.
9. Store leftover bread in an airtight container or tightly wrapped with plastic wrap on the counter for 2 to 3 days, or use a bread box.
10. Enjoy the bread buttered with hot soups and stews or dipped in Hot Pie's Gravy (page 12).

“*You've got nothing to fear from us, son. The lords of Westeros want to burn the countryside. We're trying to save it. Now come on. We'll talk some more over brown bread and stew. And then you can go on your way.*

THOROS OF MYR”

V • YIELD: 6 TO 8 DIREWOLF BISCUITS • PREP TIME: 1 HOUR
REST TIME: 30 MINUTES • COOKING TIME: 15 MINUTES • DIFFICULTY: MODERATE

HOT PIE'S DIREWOLF BREAD

Direwolves, ravens, and dragons were popular figures made from Westerosi oaten bread, a tradition said to have begun in the days of King Joffrey Baratheon when a baker's apprentice, employed at the Inn at the Crossroads, began making them for patrons and friends. The biscuitlike bread—sometimes called oat cake—was sweetened according to taste and paired well with cheese, butter, and Northern Ale Preserves (page 14). More intensely sugared biscuits were often carried in travelers' packs and eaten with a warm drink, such as Hot Spiced Cider (page 79).

1 cup quick-cooking oats

1 cup all-purpose flour

¾ cup whole-wheat flour

1 teaspoon baking powder

¼ teaspoon fine salt

1 teaspoon Westerosi Sweet Spice (page 11)

⅓ cup dark brown sugar (or less, as desired)

¾ cup unsalted butter

1 large egg, lightly beaten

1 tablespoon honey

1 tablespoon milk (or as needed)

1. Preheat the oven to 350°F. Line a baking sheet with parchment paper.
2. In a large mixing bowl, add the oats, flours, baking powder, salt, Westerosi Sweet Spice, and brown sugar. Stir to combine.
3. With a pastry cutter or clean hands, cut or rub in the butter until it resembles coarse bread crumbs about the size of peas.
4. Add in the beaten egg and honey, and use a rubber spatula to form a dough. If necessary, add in a tablespoon of milk until the dough holds together easily and is pliable but not wet.
5. Divide the dough into 2 halves. Wrap each half in plastic wrap, and chill for 30 minutes to 1 hour.
6. Take out one portion of dough. On a lightly floured surface, with a lightly floured rolling pin, roll out the dough to about a ⅜-inch thickness.
7. Shape the dough into a direwolf using a template or a screenshot for reference, using a knife to cut the finer details. Reroll the excess to create another direwolf. Repeat until you run out of dough; generally, this makes 3 to 4 direwolves. Repeat with the second portion of dough.
8. Carefully transfer each direwolf to the parchment-lined baking sheet, placing them about an inch apart.
9. Bake for 10 to 15 minutes until the edges are lightly browned.
10. Remove the cookie sheet from the oven. Let the direwolves cool on the baking sheet for 5 minutes. Then use a spatula to carefully transfer them to a wire rack to cool completely.

TEMPLATE ON PAGE 185

"Well, I made you something."

HOT PIE

THOROS'S BLACKSTRAP RUM

Thoros of Myr was a Red Priest of the Lord of Light, remembered for his fearlessness in battle, flaming sword of wildfire, and fondness for rum. His powers of pyrokinesis and resurrection were legendary, and his heroism in the war on the wights was commemorated in a fiery spiced drink.

1 tablespoon dark brown sugar

1 teaspoon lime juice, plus more for the rim

1 tablespoon blackstrap molasses

1 ounce Cherry Heering or cherry brandy

2 to 4 dashes molasses or orange bitters (optional)

2 to 3 ounces blackstrap rum or other black rum

Ground cinnamon, for garnish (optional)

Freshly grated nutmeg, for garnish (optional)

1. Spread the brown sugar around the bottom of a shallow bowl.
2. In a separate shallow bowl, add enough lime juice or water to just cover the bottom of the bowl.
3. Dip the rim of a heat-resistant glass, such as a thick glass mug, in the lime juice. Place the glass upside down in the brown sugar, and rotate it so the sugar sticks to the rim.
4. In the serving glass, stir together the molasses, Cherry Heering, lime juice, and bitters in hot water until it all dissolves.
5. Hold a spoon over the surface of the drink, and slowly pour on the rum, letting the spoon overflow so that the rum settles on top.
6. Sprinkle the drink with cinnamon and nutmeg.
7. Carefully ignite the top layer of rum with a long-necked lighter, and let it burn for a few seconds. To extinguish, place a large bowl or a larger glass over the entire drink, to suffocate the flames.
8. Give the drink a stir. Drink warm, or add ice and serve cold.

> *Not easy finding molasses in wartime.*
>
> THOROS OF MYR

GUEST RITES (BREAD AND SALT)

Guest rites were widespread in the noble houses of the Seven Kingdoms. Platters of Bread and Salt, representing the necessities of life, were offered to guests as a greeting and to honor them under the host's roof. Whether high- or low-born, the rite ensured safety—of both host and guest—throughout the stay.

This rite was most cruelly violated by Lord Walder Frey of House Frey at the wedding of his daughter, Roslin Frey, to Lord Edmure Tully. Lord Frey acted out of revenge, after King of the North Robb Stark broke a marriage pact between their houses. The massacre of the Stark guests and their bannermen led the folk of the North to wonder what vengeance the gods might wreak upon the Freys for their transgression. They named the atrocity "The Red Wedding."

The warm, butter-infused loaves, or rastons, of this traditional recipe can be pulled apart and used for salt dipping. Alternatively, they can serve as bowls, or trenchers, for the welcome repast.

2 tablespoons granulated sugar

1 cup ale, warmed (choose a sweeter, less hoppy ale)

1 packet (¾ tablespoon) active dry yeast

2 large eggs, lightly beaten

1 teaspoon fine salt

3½ cups all-purpose flour

1 egg yolk, lightly beaten, for brushing

1 tablespoon milk or cream, for brushing

¾ cup unsalted butter, melted

Finishing salt, to taste

> *My honored guests, be welcome within my walls and at my table. I extend to you my hospitality and protection in the light of the Seven.*
>
> WALDER FREY

1. In a medium mixing bowl, whisk the sugar into the ale. Stir in the yeast, and let it sit for 10 minutes until bubbly. Whisk in the eggs.
2. In a separate large mixing bowl, sift together the salt and flour. Add in the ale mixture, and stir to combine. If the mixture is too dry to come together, add a tad more ale or some milk.
3. When the dough comes together, turn it out onto a very lightly floured surface. Knead until the dough is smooth, and shape it into a ball. If it's too sticky to shape, add a bit more flour. Place the dough in a greased bowl, and cover with plastic wrap or a slightly damp cloth. Allow the dough to rise until it has doubled in size, approximately 1 hour. Note that the ambient temperature and humidity in your home, as well as your elevation, all affect how fast the dough rises. The time it takes to double in size can vary. It might take longer in Winterfell than King's Landing!
4. When the dough has doubled in size, punch it down. Once again, turn it out onto a lightly floured surface. Divide the dough into 2 equal pieces, and form them into round loaves. Place the loaves on a parchment-lined baking tray, and allow them to rise for another 15 to 20 minutes.
5. Preheat the oven to 400°F. In a small bowl, whisk together the extra egg yolk and milk.
6. When the dough has risen, brush the loaves with the extra egg yolk and milk. Sprinkle with the coarse salt, and then score the top of the loaves in a cross shape. Bake in the oven for 20 to 25 minutes until the bread is golden brown in color and sounds hollow when tapped on the bottom. Transfer the bread to a wire rack to cool.
7. After the loaves have cooled enough to handle, cut a circle around the top of the loaf and remove the "lid." Pull out the insides, tear them into pieces, and place them into a bowl. Pour the melted butter over the crumbs, and mix together with a spoon.
8. Return the crumbs and any remaining butter to the hollow loaves, and place the lid back on. Warm in the oven for another 4 to 5 minutes before serving. To perform guest rites, dip the butter-soaked pieces into a very small amount of finishing salt before eating.

GF • YIELD: 4 TO 6 SERVINGS • PREP TIME: 30 MINUTES
COOKING TIME: 45 MINUTES • REST TIME: 14-25 HOURS • DIFFICULTY: MODERATE

THE HOUND'S WHOLE CHICKEN

Roast chicken was served Riverlands style at noble tables, inns, and farmsteads across the kingdom. Seasoned with salt and spices and marinated in buttermilk, it was served oven fresh, without accompaniment. Many diners considered the crisp, golden skin and soft, flaky meat to be "food of the gods."

1 whole chicken (3 to 4 pounds)

2 tablespoons salt (or to taste), divided

2 cups buttermilk

6 garlic cloves, minced

2 tablespoons honey

3 to 4 tablespoons Northern Strong Spices (page 11), divided

PAIRS WELL WITH:

Kingswood Bramble Saucc (page 14) or Hot Pie's Gravy (page 12)

> *Think I'll take two chickens.*
>
> THE HOUND

1. Remove any gizzards and other organs from the cavity, if present. Season the chicken with 1 tablespoon salt, and let it sit for at least 1 hour (or up to overnight) in the fridge.
2. In a medium mixing bowl, whisk together the remaining salt, buttermilk, garlic, honey, and 2 tablespoons of the spices.
3. Place the chicken in a gallon-size sealable freezer bag, and pour in the buttermilk mixture. Seal the bag, and press the buttermilk all around the chicken. If the chicken won't fit into a gallon bag, place the chicken in a large mixing bowl, breast side down, and cover with plastic wrap.
4. Place the bag or bowl on a rimmed plate, and refrigerate for at least 12 hours and up to 24 hours. Rotate the bag periodically to ensure that every part of the chicken is marinated.
5. An hour or 2 before before you cook the chicken, remove it from the bag and thoroughly pat it dry with paper towels. Rub the chicken with the remaining spices and, if desired, tie the legs together with twine. Let it come to room temperature outside the refrigerator for 1 to 2 hours.
6. Preheat the oven to 475°F. Preheat a 10-inch cast-iron skillet or a shallow roasting pan over medium heat. Wipe the chicken with paper towels once again, and then place the chicken, breast side up, in the pan. It should sizzle.
7. Place the pan in the center of the oven, and watch for it to start browning within the first 20 minutes. The skin should begin to blister, but if the skin is getting too brown before it is cooked through or begins to char or smoke at any point, drape it with aluminum foil and reduce the temperature by 25°F.
8. When the chicken has been roasting for about 30 minutes, flip the chicken over. Roast it for another 10 to 20 minutes, and then flip the chicken back over to crisp the skin on the breast, about another 5 to 10 minutes; the chicken should be browned all over, with the internal temperature in the thickest part of the thigh reading 160°F and the juices running clear.
9. Transfer the chicken to a platter, and let it rest for 10 minutes before carving and serving. Or eat it with your bare hands!

GF* • YIELD: 4–6 SERVINGS • PREP TIME: 30 MINUTES
REST TIME: 30 MINUTES • COOKING TIME: 2 HOURS • DIFFICULTY: MODERATE

RABBIT STEW

Rabbits were valued in Westeros, bred for fur to line winter garments and for their delicious meat. The lean flesh was commonly eaten by smallfolk in stews, with field mushrooms, garden herbs, and apple cider vinegar. The fragrant sauce infused the meat with flavor and added tenderness to the lean meat.

- 2 ounces dried wild or porcini mushrooms
- 2 to 3 pounds rabbit meat, cleaned and cut into pieces (or use chicken thighs and legs)
- 1 to 2 teaspoons salt (or to taste)
- 2 teaspoons Old Valyrian Blend (page 11)
- 6 to 7 strips thick-cut bacon, diced
- ⅓ cup all-purpose flour
- 2 sprigs fresh rosemary
- 4 sprigs fresh thyme
- 2 bay leaves
- 4 shallots, sliced
- 4 garlic cloves, minced
- 16 ounces fresh mushrooms
- 1 tablespoon unsalted butter (or as needed)
- 1 tablespoon apple cider vinegar
- 2 cups white wine
- 2 cups chicken broth
- 2 tablespoons apple or apricot jelly
- 2 tablespoons chopped flat-leaf parsley, plus more for garnish

1. Rinse the dried mushrooms to remove any grit, and soak them in 2 cups hot water. Set aside.
2. Season the rabbit with the salt and Old Valyrian Blend. Let sit at room temperature for 30 to 60 minutes.
3. Cook the bacon in a Dutch oven over medium-high heat until crisp, about 6 to 8 minutes. Remove the bacon pieces with a slotted spoon, and set aside. Reserve the fat in the pot.
4. Toss the rabbit pieces with the flour until coated, shaking off any excess. Cook the rabbit in the bacon fat over medium-high heat until browned. You may need to work in batches, to prevent crowding. Remove the browned pieces to a rimmed plate, and set aside.
5. Roughly chop the rehydrated mushrooms, reserving both the mushrooms and the soaking liquid. Using kitchen twine, tie together the rosemary, thyme, and bay leaves. Set aside both the mushrooms and the herbs.
6. To the same pan you used to cook the meat, add the shallots; sauté for 2 to 3 minutes until translucent. Add the garlic, and cook for another minute until fragrant. Add the fresh mushrooms, and cook for 5 to 6 more minutes or until the mushrooms are browned and softened. If you run out of bacon fat at any point, add butter as needed.
7. Add the vinegar, and scrape up any browned bits from the bottom of the pan.
8. To the Dutch oven, add the rehydrated mushrooms and soaking liquid, the white wine, the chicken broth, the meat, and most of the bacon (reserve some for garnishing, if desired). Bring to a low boil over medium-high heat. Once boiling, reduce heat to low; add the herb bundle and jelly, and stir.
9. Simmer on low for 90 minutes until the meat is falling off the bone. Ten minutes before it's done, adjust the seasonings to taste and add in the parsley.
10. Garnish with additional parsley and bacon, if desired, and serve hot.

> *There's a storm coming. You'll be wanting a roof tonight. There's fresh hay in the barn. And Sally here makes rabbit stew just like her mom used to do. We don't have much, but any man that bled for House Tully is welcome to it.*
>
> FARMER HAMLET

V, V+*, GF • YIELD: 8–10 SERVINGS • PREP TIME: 20 MINUTES
COOKING TIME: 1 HOUR • DIFFICULTY: EASY

CANDIED ALMONDS

Candied almonds were a crunchy sweet made for young nobles by indulgent castle cooks. Bags of the white-fleshed nuts came from Essos and Dorne and were stirred into a sugared cinnamon mix before they were baked till crisp in the kitchen ovens.

¾ cup granulated sugar

1 tablespoon ground cinnamon

1 large egg white (no yolk)

1 tablespoon vanilla paste or extract

1 to 2 teaspoons rose water (or to taste)

16 ounces (about 3½ cups) raw almonds

Coarse salt

1. Preheat the oven to 250°F. Generously grease a large rimmed baking sheet with butter.
2. In a small bowl, whisk together the sugar and cinnamon. Set aside.
3. In a large mixing bowl, vigorously whip the egg white, vanilla, and rose water with a whisk until foamy, about 1 to 2 minutes.
4. Add the almonds to the egg mixture, and stir until evenly coated.
5. Stir the cinnamon sugar into the almond mixture until the almonds are evenly coated. Use a rubber spatula to scrape any cinnamon sugar off the sides of the bowl and into the almonds.
6. Spread the almonds in a single layer on the prepared baking sheet.
7. Bake for 1 hour, using a spatula to mix them around about every 15 minutes.
8. Remove from the oven, and stir once more. Let cool on the baking sheet for at least 15 minutes before serving.
9. Store in an airtight container at room temperature for up to 2 to 3 weeks, or in the freezer for up to 2 months.

> *Your mother always had a sweet tooth, you know . . . at suppertime, she would always go straight for honey cakes, candied almonds, custard . . .*
>
> LYSA ARRYN

V • YIELD: 6 TO 8 CAKES • PREP TIME: 45 MINUTES
COOKING TIME: 45 MINUTES • DIFFICULTY: MODERATE

HONEY CAKES

Light, spiced cakes made with butter and brown sugar were served steeped in a sticky honey sauce. The sweet confections were much loved as a winter pudding in Riverrun.

CAKES

¾ cup unsalted butter, plus more for greasing

1 cup all-purpose flour

1 teaspoon baking powder

¼ teaspoon baking soda

1 teaspoon fine salt

1 teaspoon Westerosi Sweet Spice (page 11)

1 teaspoon orange zest

¾ cup light brown sugar

3 large eggs, lightly beaten

¼ cup whole milk

SYRUP AND TOPPING

1 cup honey

¼ cup granulated sugar (or to taste)

¾ cup water

1 cinnamon stick (optional)

1 teaspoon lemon juice

Sliced almonds, for topping

1. Preheat the oven to 350°F. Grease six to eight 4-inch cake pans or ramekins with butter, and set them on a rimmed baking sheet. Alternatively, you can use 2 muffin tins.
2. To make the syrup, combine the honey, sugar, water, and cinnamon stick in a medium saucepan. Bring to a simmer over medium-high heat, and simmer for 5 minutes. Stir in the lemon juice, bring to a boil, and cook for 2 more minutes. Set aside.
3. In a medium mixing bowl, sift together the flour, baking powder, baking soda, salt, and Westerosi Sweet Spice. Stir in the orange zest. Set aside.
4. In a large mixing bowl, cream together the butter and brown sugar until light and fluffy. Beat in the eggs, one at a time. Beat in the flour mixture, alternating with the milk; mix just until incorporated.
5. Pour the batter into the greased cake pans.
6. Transfer the cakes to the preheated oven, and bake for 25 to 35 minutes or until a toothpick inserted into the center of one of the middle cakes comes out clean. Allow to cool for 5 to 10 minutes in the pan.
7. Use a toothpick to poke some holes in the cakes. Then pour honey syrup over the cakes, allowing the syrup to steep into the cakes. Sprinkle the cakes with the slivered almonds, allow to cool and steep for another 10 minutes, and then serve.

V • YIELD: 6 TO 8 SERVINGS • PREP TIME: 20 MINUTES
COOKING TIME: 15 MINUTES • REST TIME: 2 HOURS • DIFFICULTY: MODERATE

MOON CUSTARD

Housc Arryn's fortress lay in rugged country and was built atop a peak in the Mountains of the Moon. The stronghold's High Hall, seat of the Lord of the Vale, was constructed with a circular door in the floor known as the Moon Door. Through this door, enemies of House Arryn were thrown to their death.

The door's terrifying reputation was cclcbratcd by cooks throughout Westeros with moon-shape cream puddings flavored with honey, thyme, and other mountain herbs and flowers. The color was said to resemble the pale faces of the condemned, and the quivering consistency represented their terrified quaking during the moments before they were ejected from the door.

2½ cups whole milk
1 cup heavy cream
½ cup honey (or to taste)
2 cinnamon sticks
1 chamomile tea bag
1 to 2 sprigs fresh thyme
2 teaspoons vanilla extract
6 egg yolks
¼ cup potato or corn starch
½ teaspoon nutmeg (optional)
Ground cinnamon, for garnish (optional)
Sliced almonds, for garnish (optional)

PAIRS WELL WITH:

Fresh berries or Poached Pears (page 25)

1. Add the milk, cream, honey, cinnamon sticks, tea, thyme, and vanilla extract to a medium saucepan. Heat until the honey dissolves and the mixture begins to simmer, but do not boil or scald the milk. Remove from heat, and cover.
2. Whisk together the egg yolks, potato or corn starch, and nutmeg in a medium mixing bowl.
3. Remove the cinnamon stick, thyme sprig, and tea bag from the hot milk mixture. While whisking constantly, slowly pour the hot milk mixture into the egg yolk and starch mixture. Continue to whisk until fully incorporated
4. Transfer the custard base back into the saucepan, and heat over medium-low heat. Continue to whisk gently until the custard thickens to a thick, puddinglike consistency, about 4 to 6 minutes. Be sure to scrape the edges, sides, and bottom of the pan frequently to heat the custard evenly and prevent it from "setting" on the sides and bottom of the saucepan.
5. Let the custard cool for 5 minutes. Transfer to ramekins, molds, or heatproof serving cups. Cover with plastic wrap, and let the custards set in the refrigerator for at least 2 hours (ideally, overnight).
6. If using a mold, fill a shallow pan with boiling water. Let the mold sit in the boiling water to help release the custard, making sure no water makes contact with the custard. Place the serving plate on top of the mold, and flip it over so the custard releases onto the plate.
7. Garnish with cinnamon and sliced almonds, and serve.

YIELD: 6 TO 8 SERVINGS • PREP TIME: 45 MINUTES
COOKING TIME: 4 HOURS (MOSTLY IDLE) • DIFFICULTY: ADVANCED

KIDNEY PIE

The best chefs of Westeros knew that the king of kidneys was that of the calf. Small, tender, and with an exquisite flavor, calf kidneys were ordered from butchers and used fresh the same day, baked into a pie with bottom round steak. Some cooks made it meaty, and some used a thick gravy: The gravy pie was a speciality of the Crossroads Inn, a hostelry once famed for its excellent cuisine.

PIE

- 2 pounds bottom round or beef chuck, cut into 2-inch pieces
- 4 to 5 ounces calf kidneys, diced (or use 8 ounces sliced mushrooms or ½ cup cooked red kidney beans, drained)
- Salt
- Black pepper
- 1 to 2 tablespoons Old Valyrian Blend (page 11)
- 4 ounces pancetta or ½ cup chopped bacon
- 1 large yellow onion, chopped
- 4 garlic cloves, minced
- 2 medium carrots, chopped
- 1 to 2 tablespoons tomato paste (optional)
- 1 tablespoon Dijon mustard
- 2 tablespoons Worcestershire sauce
- 1½ cups dark beer or ale
- 1½ cups beef broth
- 1 to 2 tablespoons honey
- 2 bay leaves

1. Preheat the oven to 275°F. Season the beef with salt and pepper.
2. Pat the beef and kidneys (if using) dry, and generously season with salt, pepper, and Old Valyrian Blend. Set aside.
3. On a lightly floured surface, shape the dough into 2 circles. The larger portion of dough should be about 14 inches in diameter, and the second portion should be about 8 inches in diameter. Wrap these in plastic wrap, and set aside in the fridge.
4. In a large skillet, cook the pancetta or bacon over medium-high heat until crisp. Remove it from the skillet with a slotted spoon, but retain the fat in the pan.
5. Brown the beef in batches, flipping to brown the pieces on all sides. Remove the browned pieces, and set aside.
6. Add the onion, and sauté for 2 to 3 minutes until translucent. Add the garlic, and cook for another minute until fragrant. Add the carrots and the mushrooms (if using as a substitute), and cook for another 4 to 5 minutes until the carrots soften slightly and the mushrooms start to brown. Add the tomato paste and mustard, and cook for another minute.
7. Add the Worcestershire sauce to the Dutch oven, and use a wooden spoon to scrape up any browned bits remaining on the bottom.
8. Add the meat and bacon back in; then pour over the dark beer or ale, broth, and honey. Add the bay leaves. Give everything a stir. Cover, and braise in the oven for 1 hour; then add the kidneys (or kidney beans) into the stew, and braise for 1 more hour.
9. Test the liquid. The broth/gravy needs to be thick enough to coat a spoon. If it's still too thin after braising, don't give up! Transfer the Dutch oven to the stove, and heat on medium heat until reduced, about 10 to 20 minutes. Mix together the butter and flour until smooth, and then stir that into the sauce and continue to heat for another couple minutes until the sauce becomes as thick as gravy. Taste, and adjust seasoning as desired. Set aside.

Continued on page 106

> *A good kidney pie is all about the ingredients. Flour, lard, water, eggs, milk. Easy enough. But the meat, peacetime or not, getting your hands on a good bottom round steak and calves' kidneys is not easy. I mean, some people settle for plain old beef kidneys. Got no right to cook anything, them. Oh, and the gravy. Don't get me started on the gravy.*
>
> HOT PIE

1 Flaky Crust (page 9)

1 egg, lightly beaten, for washing

1 tablespoon milk

Hot Pie's Gravy (page 12), for gravy lovers (optional)

GRAVY THICKENER

2 tablespoons flour

2 tablespoons unsalted butter or lard, softened

10. Turn up the oven heat to 400°F. Remove the pie crusts you rolled out earlier from the refrigerator. Grease a 10-inch deep-dish pie plate. You can also use a small cast-iron skillet or an 8-inch springform pan.
11. Line the pie plate with the larger round of pastry, pressing it down into the bottom and sides. Crimp the edges of the crust about an inch in between each indentation. Ladle the filling into the crust until full. Place the smaller dough disk on top.
12. In a small bowl, whisk together the milk and egg. Generously brush the top and sides of the pastry with the egg wash, and season the pastry with coarse salt and pepper.
13. Bake the pie for about 30 to 35 minutes or until the top is nicely browned. Let cool for 10 to 15 minutes before serving.

NOTE: *To make Old Nan's version, skip the carrots and add ½ cup peas, 15 to 20 pearl onions, and up to 1 teaspoon Northern Strong Spices (page 11) to the filling just before you spoon it into the crust.*

EYRIE LEMON CAKES

Lemons were first brought to the Vale of Arryn in the reign of King Tommen, when the cooks of the Eyrie sought to please exiled Sansa Stark with her favorite cake. The kitchen was tasked with preparing a rich and fragrant butter cake in imitation of the cakes in the capital. The mix was baked in ramekins, and the small cakes were topped with sharp and creamy lemon curd.

CAKES

¾ cup unsalted butter, softened

4 ounces cream cheese, softened

1 cup granulated sugar

2 teaspoons vanilla extract

3 eggs

1½ cups all-purpose flour

½ teaspoon baking powder

½ teaspoon fine salt

1½ tablespoons lemon zest

TOPPING

½ cup premade lemon curd, chilled

2 lemon slices, quartered

1. Preheat the oven to 350°F. Grease six 4-inch ramekins or mini cake pans.
2. Add the butter, cream cheese, and sugar into a large mixing bowl. Using a hand mixer, beat until light and fluffy.
3. Add in the vanilla extract and the eggs, one at a time, mixing after each addition.
4. In a separate smaller mixing bowl, whisk together the flour, baking powder, salt, and lemon zest.
5. With the mixer on low speed, gradually add the flour mixture to the butter mixture until smooth.
6. Divide the batter among the prepared ramekins or cake pans.
7. Bake for about 20 minutes or until a toothpick inserted into the center comes out clean.
8. Cool the cakes in the pan for 10 minutes. Then transfer the cakes to a wire rack to cool completely.
9. To decorate, add the lemon curd to a piping bag or plastic bag with the edge cut off. Use a small spoon or melon ball scoop to take out a piece of cake from the center of each cake. Pipe or spoon some of the cold lemon curd, filling the hole completely and adding some extra on top.
10. Garnish each cake with a lemon slice quarter resting on the lemon curd.

> *Petyr had three crates brought all the way from King's Landing. He knew you liked lemon cakes. He's so kind. He really cares for you. Think where you'd be without him. In their clutches and tried for murder.*
>
> LYSA ARRYN

YIELD: 8 TO 10 SERVINGS • PREP TIME: 30 MINUTES
COOKING TIME: 2 HOURS • REST TIME: 20 MINUTES • DIFFICULTY: MODERATE

MINCED FREY PIE

Revenge is a dish that's best served cold, according to the old saying. Ayra Stark's revenge on Lord of the Crossing Walder Frey for orchestrating the killing of her mother, her brother, and his new wife and bannermen was quite the opposite: It took the form of a steaming thick-crust meat pie.

Wearing a mask from the Hall of Faces, Ayra served the pie to a complaining Frey as he questioned the whereabouts of his two sons. When Frey realized in horror that his sons were not only at the repast, but *were* the repast, Ayra slit his throat.

This pie, made with ground pork, sausage, and bacon, was made by Riverland cooks to commemorate Ayra's bravery and the welcome fall of House Frey.

- 1 Strong Crust (page 10)
- 1 pound minced pork shoulder or ground pork
- 1 pound pork sausage (no casings)
- 4 to 6 slices thick-cut bacon, chopped
- 2 tart apples, peeled, cored, and diced
- 1 large yellow onion, finely chopped
- 6 ounces butternut squash, diced
- 3 ounces chicken or pork liver pâté or liverwurst (optional)
- ¾ cup bread crumbs
- ½ cup finely chopped walnuts, pistachios, or pine nuts
- 2 large eggs, lightly beaten, plus another egg for washing
- 2 tablespoons milk or cream
- 2 tablespoons brown sugar
- 1 to 2 tablespoons Old Valyrian Blend (page 11)
- 2 teaspoons dried sage
- 2 teaspoons fine salt (or to taste)
- 1 teaspoon black pepper (or to taste)

1. Preheat the oven to 425°F. Grease an 8-inch springform pan.
2. In a large mixing bowl, combine all ingredients except the crust until well combined.
3. On a lightly floured surface, roll out the larger portion of the dough to a 12-inch circle. Carefully transfer the dough to the pan, and press it into the sides and bottoms of the pan, trimming the excess but leaving some overhang. Set aside.
4. Transfer the mixture to the prepared pie pan, and smooth it out as best you can with a rubber spatula.
5. Roll out the smaller portion of pie dough to a 10-inch circle. Carefully transfer the circle to the top of the pie, smushing the edges together to seal. Use a sharp knife to cut a hole in the center of the top crust, to allow steam to escape.
6. Brush the egg wash generously over the top of the pie. Place the springform pan on a baking sheet to catch any leakage, and transfer the pie to the lower center rack of the oven.
7. Bake at 425°F for 30 minutes; then reduce the heat to 325°F, and bake for another 80 to 90 minutes or until the internal temperature reaches at least 185°F in the center and the crust is golden brown. Check on the pie periodically. When it is nicely golden, tent the pie with aluminum foil, to prevent the top and edges from burning during the remainder of the baking time.
8. Remove the pie from the oven, and let cool for 20 to 30 minutes before releasing it from the pan. Let the pie continue to cool to almost room temperature before slicing and serving with Northern Ale Preserves, Hot Pie's Gravy, or Kingswood Bramble Sauce.

PAIRS WELL WITH:

Northern Ale Preserves (page 14), Hot Pie's Gravy (page 12), or Kingswood Bramble Sauce (page 14)

> *Where are my damn moron sons? Black Walder and Lothar promised to be here by midday.*
>
> WALDER FREY

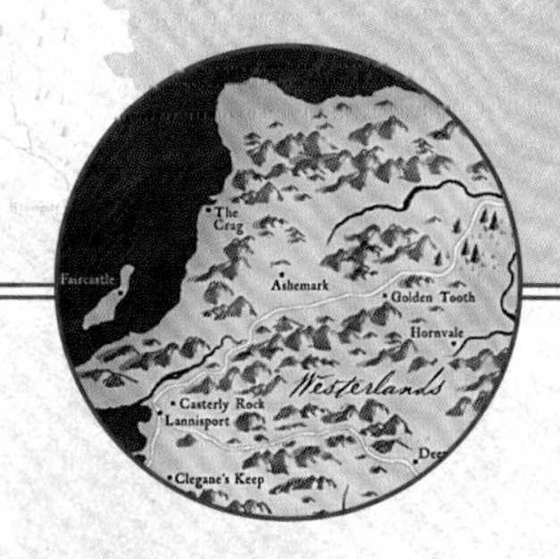

THE WESTERLANDS & THE IRON ISLANDS

The hills of the Westerlands were known more for their gold and silver mines than their agriculture, but with wealth came plenty: What could not be grown or raised in the region could be bought. This was not so for the Iron Islanders, whose austere lives on the rocky coast were sustained by a diet of fish and grog.

HONEYED WINE

No food was too fine for the Royal Hunt in the Kingswood during King Viserys's reign, and vintners sent wine from across the Seven Kingdoms in honor of Prince Aegon Targaryen's second nameday celebrations. Honeyed wine from the west-coast city of Lannisport was the pride of the Lannisters, and they drank it freely throughout the revelries.

HONEY SYRUP

½ cup honey

½ cup water

DRINK

6 ounces brandy

3 ounces honey syrup

2 ounces lemon juice

12 to 16 ounces dry mead or a sweet white wine, chilled

Lemon wheels, for garnish (optional)

1. Heat the honey and water in a small saucepan over medium heat. Stir until the honey has fully dissolved. Allow the syrup to cool. Use immediately, or transfer to a sealable container and store in the refrigerator for up to 4 weeks.
2. Add the brandy, honey syrup, lemon juice, and mead or wine to a cocktail shaker filled with ice. Shake vigorously for 10 to 15 minutes until well chilled. Strain into 2 serving glasses.
3. Add ice, if desired, and garnish with a lemon wheel.

> *The finest honeyed wine you'll ever taste—made in Lannisport, of course.*
>
> JASON LANNISTER

GF* • YIELD: 6 TO 8 SERVINGS • PREP TIME: 45 MINUTES
COOKING TIME: 45 MINUTES • DIFFICULTY: MODERATE

TURTLE STEW

Mock turtle stew was made in imitation of the once popular delicacy green turtle stew. This Westerlands staple, a meaty meal in a bowl, was served with soured cream and bread.

MEATBALLS

1½ pounds ground veal or ground beef

¼ cup pancetta

2 teaspoons Old Valyrian Blend (page 11)

1 to 2 teaspoons Westerosi Sweet Spice (page 11)

½ cup bread crumbs

2 tablespoons milk

1 large egg

1 teaspoon salt

½ teaspoon black pepper

STEW

¼ cup unsalted butter, divided

1 large red onion, sliced

4 garlic cloves, minced

2 ribs celery, chopped

2 carrots, chopped

8 ounces oyster mushrooms, sliced

2 tablespoons all-purpose flour

2 cups beef broth

1 cup Madeira wine or dry sherry

2 tablespoons Worcestershire sauce

4 sprigs fresh thyme

2 dried bay leaves

1 teaspoon lemon zest

¼ cup lemon juice

½ cup fresh parsley, chopped, plus more for garnish

Sour cream or crème fraîche, for garnish

Lemon slices, for garnish

Salt

Black pepper

1. Preheat the oven to 400°F. Line a rimmed baking sheet with parchment paper.
2. In a large mixing bowl, mix together all the meatball ingredients. Form into 1-inch meatballs, continuing until you run out of meat. Line them up 1 inch apart on the prepared baking sheet. Bake for 20 to 25 minutes. Remove the baking sheet from the oven, and set aside.
3. In a Dutch oven, melt 2 tablespoons of the butter over medium-high heat. Sauté the onion for 2 to 3 minutes until translucent. Add the garlic, and cook for another minute until fragrant. Add the celery, carrots, and mushrooms. Continue to sauté until the vegetables soften and the mushrooms brown, about 6 to 7 minutes, seasoning with salt and pepper to taste. Remove the veggies from the pot, and set aside.
4. To the Dutch oven, add the remaining butter and melt it; sprinkle in the flour. Cook the roux for 5 to 6 minutes until it turns light brown, stirring constantly to prevent burning.
5. Pour in the beef broth, wine or sherry, and Worcestershire sauce, stirring to combine. Bring to a boil, and then reduce heat to low.
6. Using kitchen twine, tie together the thyme and bay leaves, and add this to the Dutch oven, along with the meatballs and sautéed veggies. Give everything a stir.
7. Simmer for 20 to 30 minutes until the meatballs and veggies are tender. Add in the lemon zest, lemon juice, and parsley, and cook for another 10 minutes. Taste, and adjust seasoning as desired.
8. Garnish each bowl with crème fraîche, lemon slices, and a sprinkling of parsley. Serve hot.

> *When I was twelve, I milked my eel into a pot of turtle stew.*
>
> TYRION LANNISTER

GINGERBREAD CASTLES

Westerlands gingerbread was made using crystalized ginger and mixed spices combined in a dark molasses cake. The mini bundt pans used to bake the cakes lent the gingerbread the look of tiny castles. These "gingerbread castles" were a child's fantasy. Among those who had never seen a castle, they were hungry imaginings that they could live in a noble world of cake. The gingerbread also inspired a phrase adults used to disparage those who lived in a fantasy world "where the castles are made from gingerbread and the moats are filled with blackberry wine."

½ cup unsalted butter, softened, plus more for greasing

1¾ cups all-purpose flour

1 teaspoon baking soda

¼ teaspoon baking powder

1 tablespoon Westerosi Sweet Spice (page 11)

1 tablespoon Northern Strong Spices (page 11)

½ teaspoon fine salt

1 teaspoon orange zest (optional)

½ cup dark brown sugar (packed)

½ cup molasses, black treacle, or buckwheat honey

1 large egg, at room temperature

½ cup whole milk, divided

½ cup crystalized ginger, chopped fine

Confectioner's sugar, for dusting

1. Preheat the oven to 350°F. Grease a mini bundt pan with butter.
2. In a medium mixing bowl, whisk together the flour, baking soda, baking powder, spices, salt, and orange zest.
3. In a separate large mixing bowl, cream together the butter and brown sugar until fluffy, using a hand mixer on medium-high speed. Mix in the molasses, black treacle, or honey and the egg until the mixture looks brown and smooth; scrape the sides of the bowl with a rubber spatula, as needed.
4. With the mixer on low speed, mix in a third of the flour mixture, and alternate with half the milk; repeat until both the milk and the flour mixture are fully incorporated. Try not to overmix; mix just enough that there is no more dry flour. Once mixed, gently fold in the candied ginger pieces.
5. Distribute the batter evenly among the prepared mini bundt pan holes until each is about two-thirds full. Bake for 18 to 20 minutes or until a toothpick inserted in the middle of one of the center cakes comes out clean. Remove the cakes from the oven, and cool in the pan for 5 minutes; then transfer them to a rack to cool completely.
6. When cooled, dust with confectioner's sugar, and serve.

"*Where the castles are made of gingerbread and the moats are filled with blackberry wine. The powerful have always preyed on the powerless, that's how they became powerful in the first place.*"

TYRION LANNISTER

V, V+, GF • YIELD: 2 TO 3 SERVINGS • PREP TIME: 5 MINUTES
COOKING TIME: 10 MINUTES • DIFFICULTY: EASY

IRON ISLANDS GROG

Ironborn sailors of the west coast drank a sweetened kelp grog, spiced with rum to warm their spirits at sea and fire their ardour for battle. Kelp was considered a gift from the Drowned God, the deity worshiped by the ironborn, and it was eaten and imbibed in the god's honor.

1 piece dried kelp (kombu), or use a bag of green tea

2 whole allspice berries or cloves

2 cups water

2 tablespoons dark brown sugar (or to taste)

2 ounces lime juice

Pinch of sea salt

4 to 6 ounces aged or spiced rum

1. Add the kombu, whole spices, and water to a small saucepan. Bring to a low simmer over medium heat. When simmering, remove from heat, cover, and let rest for about 5 minutes, to allow the kombu to steep. If using green tea, add it after the water has simmered and been removed from heat.
2. Remove the kombu or green tea, and add in the brown sugar, lime juice, and sea salt. Stir until the sugar and honey dissolve.
3. To serve hot, divide the rum between two mugs, pour in the tea mixture, and serve immediately.
4. If serving cold, don't add the rum quite yet. Transfer the hot tea mixture to a sealable heatproof storage container, such as a mason jar. Cover, and put in the refrigerator to cool; it can be stored in the refrigerator for up to 3 days. When cooled, shake to redistribute the sugars, which may have separated. Divide the rum and ice between 2 serving glasses, and top with the tea mixture.

> *We are a sea people. Our god is a sea god.*
>
> YARA GREYJOY

BLACKBERRY WINE

Late summer's golden sun ripened the tart crab apples, elderberries, and plump blackberries of the Westerland valleys. Blackberries were the preferred fruit for wine making, and smallfolk made a potent punch from the autumn crop that was bottled and traded throughout the Seven Kingdoms and beyond.

1 cup fresh blackberries, plus more for garnish

1 tablespoon lemon juice

¼ cup brown sugar

½ cup blackberry brandy

1½ cups red wine

1. In a small pitcher, muddle together the blackberries, lemon juice, and brown sugar.
2. Add the blackberry brandy and red wine, and stir.
3. Refrigerate for at least 2 hours.
4. Garnish each serving with fresh blackberries.

> *It's blackberry wine. I made it myself.*
>
> LANNISTER SOLDIER

THE IMP'S DELIGHT

Tyrion Lannister of the Westerlands, Hand of King Bran I the Broken, yearned to become a vintner in the days before his destiny was revealed. His long tenure and many achievements as Hand were commemorated as he would have wished: in drink, with a rum, brandy, and sweet Lannisport wine aperitif. Some dusted the drink with gold, to show that riches and power were no substitute for good food and fine wine.

1 ounce white rum

1 ounce peach or apricot brandy

1 ounce pomegranate juice

¼ ounce lemon juice

2 to 3 drops aromatic bitters (optional)

Pinch of gold edible luster dust (optional)

3 to 4 ounces port wine, chilled

Dehydrated lemon wheel or skewered fruit, for garnish

1. Add the rum, brandy, pomegranate juice, lemon juice, bitters, and luster dust to a cocktail shaker filled with ice.
2. Shake vigorously for 10 to 15 seconds until well chilled.
3. Strain into a serving glass.
4. Top with port wine.
5. Garnish with a lemon wheel or skewered fruit, and serve.

> *Yes, yes. Fermentation. One day, after our queen has taken the Seven Kingdoms . . . I'd like to have my own vineyard. Make my own wine. The Imp's Delight. Only my close friends could drink it.*
>
> TYRION LANNISTER

FISH CAKES

Skillet fried cakes of thick-flaked fish with hens' eggs and garden herbs were an Iron Islands speciality. They were flavored with barrel-aged fish sauce and served with salty samphire or rough brown bread, all of it gathered and made by thralls, the slaves procured by ironborn raiders. Generations of ironborn grew up on the dish, and for sailors on distant seas, the seared patties were a taste of home.

CAKES

1 pound cooked fish (such as cod, crab, or salmon), flaked

2 cups cold mashed potatoes

Salt

Black pepper

1 cup panko bread crumbs

2 large eggs, lightly beaten

¼ cup fresh parsley, chopped, plus more for garnish

2 tablespoons minced chives

1 to 2 tablespoons patis or fish sauce (or use Worcestershire sauce)

1 tablespoon Dijon or spicy brown mustard

2 tablespoons Old Valyrian Blend (page 11)

¼ teaspoon nutmeg

1 tablespoon milk, or as needed (optional)

2 to 4 tablespoons oil, for frying

DIPPING SAUCE (OPTIONAL)

1 cup sour cream

2 tablespoons fresh dill

1 tablespoon fresh chives, chopped

2 teaspoons horseradish

1 tablespoon spicy brown mustard

Sea salt

1. To make the sauce, mix together all the ingredients in a small bowl. Taste, and adjust seasoning as desired. Set aside the sauce until serving time.
2. In a large mixing bowl, combine all the ingredients except the cooking oil. (This includes the mashed potatoes, when cooled.) If the mixture is too crumbly, add a splash of milk. If it's too wet and sticky, add more bread crumbs.
3. Shape the batter into thick, round cakes with about ¼ to ⅓ cup of batter each.
4. Heat the oil in a large skillet over medium-high heat. When the pan is hot, fry the cakes in batches, making sure they don't touch each other, until they are nicely browned on both sides—about 2 to 3 minutes per side
5. Serve warm with the dipping sauce and a sprinkling of parsley on top, if desired.

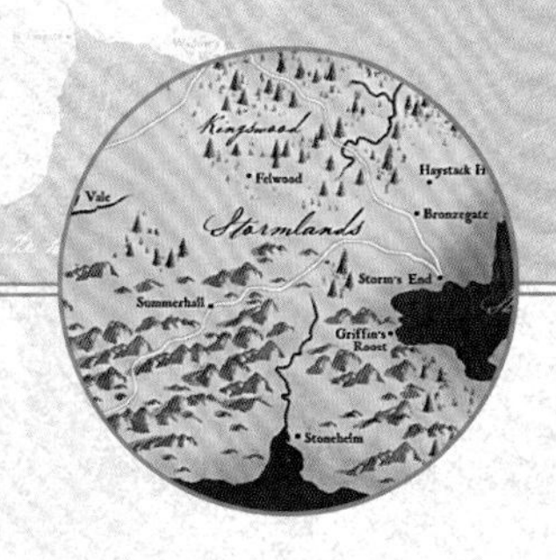

THE STORMLANDS & THE REACH

The vast, fertile lands of the Reach and its forested eastern counterpart produced what was arguably some of the finest food on the continent. The regions excelled in cake and wine, baking and fermenting an exceptional range of pastries and intoxicating liquors.

V • YIELD: 12 CAKES • PREP TIME: 30 MINUTES
COOKING TIME: 35 MINUTES • DIFFICULTY: EASY

HUNTING PARTY CAKES

Small glazed occasion cakes, lightly perfumed with orange, almond, and vanilla, and sprinkled with crushed hazelnuts, were made for serving with tea. Semolina flour was used to add to the subtle nut flavor, making these small cakes a much-loved nameday choice.

CAKES

¼ cup unsalted butter, melted and cooled, plus more for greasing

2 cups semolina flour

1 cup all-purpose flour

½ cup granulated sugar

1 teaspoon baking powder

½ teaspoon salt

2 cups whole milk

1 tablespoon orange zest

½ teaspoon almond extract (or to taste)

2 teaspoons vanilla extract

¼ cup sliced hazelnuts

GLAZE

2 tablespoons orange juice

¾ cup confectioner's sugar

1 teaspoon orange blossom water (optional)

1. Preheat the oven to 325°F. Grease a standard muffin tin with butter.
2. In a large mixing bowl, whisk together both of the flours, along with the sugar, baking powder, and salt.
3. In a smaller mixing bowl, stir together the milk, butter, orange zest, and almond and vanilla extracts.
4. Add the milk mixture to the flour mixture, and stir until the batter is smooth. The batter will be very wet initially, but it will thicken up.
5. Pour or spoon the batter into the prepared muffin tin. Sprinkle the nuts over the tops on the cakes.
6. Bake in the preheated oven for 30 to 35 minutes or until the cakes are golden and a toothpick inserted in the center of one of the middle cakes comes out clean.
7. Allow to cool in the tin for about 10 minutes; then transfer to a wire rack to cool completely.
8. Make the glaze by whisking together the orange juice, confectioner's sugar, and orange blossom water in a small bowl. Drizzle the cakes with the glaze, and let the glaze set for 5 minutes before serving.

"*And how have you served the realm of late, Lady Redwyne? By eating cake?*"

RHAENYRA TARGARYEN

V • YIELD: 12 PASTRIES • PREP TIME: 30 MINUTES
REST TIME: 30 MINUTES • COOKING TIME: 30 MINUTES • DIFFICULTY: MODERATE

SWEETMEATS WITH NUTS AND HONEY

The Red Keep's kitchen staff traveled with the court, transporting everything necessary to sustain the king's retinue by horse and cart. Bakers, pie makers, and pastry chefs wheeled small wood-fired ovens to outdoor feasts, using the clay domes to bake a steady supply of breads, scones, and pies, plus sweetmeats such as honey and pistachio scones for the banqueting tables.

3 cups all-purpose flour

½ cup granulated sugar

1 tablespoon baking powder

¾ teaspoon salt

1 teaspoon Westerosi Sweet Spice (page 11)

1 tablespoon lime zest

1 teaspoon vanilla extract

1 to 2 tablespoons rose water (or to taste)

1⅓ cup heavy cream, plus more as needed (do not substitute milk)

¼ cup honey, loosened (or to taste)

½ cup pistachios, shelled and ground or chopped fine

Raw sugar, for garnish

1. Line a large baking sheet with parchment paper.
2. In a large mixing bowl, whisk together the flour, sugar, baking powder, salt, Westerosi Sweet Spice, and lime zest.
3. Stir the vanilla and rose water into the cream. Clear a well in the center of the flour mixture, and add the cream. Fold the flour into the cream, and start to gently mix until the sides of the bowl are clean. The dough should be ever so slightly sticky and loose, not dry or stiff. If it's dry, add a tablespoon more cream, and fold it in.
4. Gather the dough into a ball, and place on a very lightly floured surface. Knead the dough a few times just until the dough holds together.
5. Divide the dough in half, and shape each into a half-circle about an inch thick and 6 to 7 inches wide. Cut each circle into 4 to 6 triangular pieces. Place the triangles on the baking sheet, alternating narrow or wide end up pointed up, with some space between each.
6. Ideally, at this point, you want to freeze the pastries for 15 to 20 minutes or refrigerate for 25 to 30 minutes before baking. However, if your refrigerator can't accommodate this, it's okay to skip this step.
7. Preheat the oven to 400°F.
8. Bake on the middle rack for about 10 to 15 minutes until the pastries are set and just beginning to brown. Remove the pasties from the oven. Using a pastry brush or the back of a spoon, generously brush the pastries with the honey. Gently press a handful of the pistachios down onto the pastry, using the honey to adhere the nuts. Sprinkle on some raw sugar, and bake for another 5 to 10 minutes or until lightly golden.
9. Cover the pastries with a kitchen cloth, and let them cool on the baking sheet for 5 to 10 minutes. Then transfer to a wire rack to cool completely.

V, V+, GF • YIELD: 1 SERVING • PREP TIME: 5 MINUTES • DIFFICULTY: EASY

WESTEROSI STRONGWINE

Wines from the abundant Arbor vineyards were drunk freely throughout Westeros and Essos, from rich reds to fragrant Arbor Gold. The island terroir, with its warm maritime climate, produced the finest wines in the Seven Kingdoms—including Westerosi strongwine, a brandy-fortified wine made to endure long sea journeys north and east. It guaranteed the aficionado post-prandial pleasure and ensured a sweet, dreamless sleep with no aftereffects.

- 1½ ounces gin
- 1 ounce sweet vermouth
- ¾ ounce Campari, Aperol, or other bittersweet aperitif
- 2 ounces red wine
- 2 to 3 dashes Angostura bitters (optional)
- Orange peel or dehydrated lemon slice, for garnish

1. Add all ingredients except the garnish to a cocktail shaker filled with ice.
2. Shake for 10 to 15 seconds until well chilled.
3. Strain into a serving glass.
4. Garish with an orange peel.

> *I miss Westerosi strongwine. It could be depended on for a few hours of peaceful oblivion.*
>
> DAEMON TARGARYEN

GF • YIELD: 12 TO 16 SERVINGS • PREP TIME: 40 MINUTES
COOKING TIME: 3 HOURS • DIFFICULTY: EASY

BORN AMIDST SALT & SMOKE

In the last terrible days before the reign of King Bran I the Broken, many of the faith of the Lord of Light looked for a savior in the ancient prophesy, written more than five millennia earlier. The prophesy claimed that a legendary champion would awaken dragons and reforge his famous sword Lightbringer—and banish the darkness. This champion was said to have been "born amidst salt and smoke," leaving many to wonder who the great hero might be. In the meantime, folk in their farmsteads ploughed fields, threshed corn, killed pigs, and cooked ham.

Stormlands salted and smoked ham could not banish darkness, but it satisfied thousands of appetites, bringing hope through the simple pleasure of eating.

- 1 fully cooked 8- to 10-pound bone-in smoked ham (butt or shank portion)
- 20 to 30 whole cloves
- ½ cup cherry preserves
- ½ cup honey
- ¼ cup orange juice
- 2 tablespoons Dijon mustard
- 1 tablespoon Northern Strong Spices (page 11)
- 1 tablespoon Westerosi Sweet Spice (page 11)

PAIRS WELL WITH:

Northern Ale Preserves (page 14) or Kingswood Bramble Sauce (page14)

1. Preheat the oven to 325°F. Prepare a large roasting pan with a grill rack.
2. Score the surface of the ham in a diamond pattern about ⅛ inch deep. Stick the whole cloves in the center of each diamond.
3. Place the ham in the roasting pan, and tent it with foil. Bake for 2 to 2½ hours—or longer, depending on the package directions.
4. Heat the cherry preserves, honey, orange juice, mustard, and spices in a small saucepan until bubbly. Cook until reduced and a bit thicker, about 10 to 15 minutes.
5. After about 2 hours of baking time, remove the foil and brush a third of the glaze on the ham. Put the ham back in the oven, and bake for another 15 to 20 minutes. Repeat until you have used all the glaze and the ham is nice and glossy.
6. Remove from the oven, and allow the ham to rest for 15 to 20 minutes before carving.

> *Born amidst salt and smoke? Is he a ham?*
>
> RENLY BARATHEON

V • YIELD: 8 TO 10 SERVINGS • PREP TIME: 90 MINUTES
COOKING TIME: 45 MINUTES • DIFFICULTY: ADVANCED

HARVEST APPLE TART

"It's as if all the bounty of the reach were gathered together and baked into one fine tart," wrote a Highgarden master chef in the year 301 AC during King Joffrey Baratheon's reign. The crisp, lemon-doused apples, set in a rose for House Tyrell on a fluffy bed of barley or oats, revealed its sweet flavor before the first cut with its warm caramel scent.

½ cup plus 2 tablespoons unsalted butter, divided, plus more for greasing

1 Sweet Crust (page 10)

3 to 4 Envy or Pink Lady apples

2 tablespoons lemon juice, plus more as needed

1 tablespoon Westerosi Sweet Spice (page 11), divided

¼ cup granulated sugar, plus more for sprinkling

1 cup flaked barley or old-fashioned oats

½ cup dark brown sugar

½ teaspoon salt

1 large egg

1 teaspoon vanilla extract

1 tablespoon all-purpose flour

1 tablespoon potato or corn starch

2 tablespoons apple jelly or apricot jam, melted

"*Hunger turns men into beasts. I'm glad House Tyrell has been able to help in this regard. They tell me 100 wagons arrive daily now from the Reach. Wheat, barley, apples. We've had a blessed harvest. And, of course, it's our duty to assist the capital in time of need.*

MARGAERY TYRELL"

1. Preheat the oven to 375°F. Using butter, grease a 9-inch tart tin with a removable bottom.
2. Roll out the Sweet Crust into an 11-inch circle, and transfer it to the tart tin, pressing it into the bottom and sides. Trim any excess. Place the crust in the fridge until it's time to assemble the tart.
3. Slice the apples around the core into 4 large pieces each. Slice the pieces into ⅛-inch-thick slices using a mandoline slicer, or do it by hand with a sharp knife and some patience. If you are doing it by hand, you might need to squeeze some lemon juice over the slices to keep them from browning while you work. Place the apple slices in a large mixing bowl, and gently toss them with the lemon juice, 1 teaspoon of the Westerosi Sweet Spice, and the granulated sugar. Let the apples macerate for 15 to 20 minutes.
4. Place the barley or oats in a blender, and pulse until they become almost a powder.
5. Add the ground barley or oats, ½ cup of the butter, the brown sugar, the salt, and the remaining spices to a medium mixing bowl. Use a hand mixer to cream it together, stopping the mixer a couple times to scrape down the sides of the bowl with a rubber spatula. Add in the egg and vanilla, and mix until thoroughly incorporated. Finally, add the flour and potato or corn starch, and mix until just combined. Use a rubber spatula to spread the mixture onto the bottom of the prepared tart crust.
6. Drain the apple slices, reserving the liquid for other purposes, if you like. Starting at the outer edge, arrange the larger apple slices, peel side up, in concentric circles around the circumference of the crust, slightly overlapping each other. Continue arranging the apple slices, working from biggest to smallest toward the center of the crust, until the pan is almost filled. Wrap the smaller slices around each other into a tight rose shape, and place it in the center of the tart. Fill in around the rose with more apple slices until the tart is tightly packed.
7. Cut the remaining 2 tablespoons of butter into small pieces, and dot the top of the tart with them. Sprinkle the tart with sugar. Bake in the center of the preheated oven until the crust is golden and the apples are just beginning to brown, about 40 to 45 minutes. If you notice the apple slices starting to burn, tent the tart with aluminum foil.
8. Brush the tart with melted apple jelly or apricot jam, and let cool completely. When cooled to room temperature, release the tart from the tin, and serve.

NOTE: *The "rose" arrangement of the apple slices represents Highgarden's sigil, but it is an entirely optional presentation. To simplify, you may arrange the apple slices in whatever pattern you like.*

V, GF • YIELD: 2 TO 4 SERVINGS • PREP TIME: 20 MINUTES
COOKING TIME: 15 MINUTES • DIFFICULTY: EASY

STUFFED FIGS

The fresh fig was a fruit beloved in Highgarden for its ripe sapidity and health-promoting effects. Cut and filled with goat's cheese or other creamy curd, figs were served in season and on demand.

- 1 dozen fresh figs
- ½ cup chèvre, mascarpone, or soft cheese of your choice
- 1 tablespoon olive oil
- Coarse salt
- Cracked black pepper
- ¼ cup chopped walnuts or pecans
- 1 to 2 tablespoons honey (or to taste)

1. Preheat the oven to 375°F. Line a rimmed baking sheet with parchment paper.
2. Use a paring knife to cut the stem off the figs. Cut an X or a cross on the top of each fig, stopping about two-thirds of the way down.
3. In the cavity you cut, add 2 teaspoons of cheese into each fig. Drizzle with olive oil and season lightly with coarse salt and cracked black pepper.
4. Place the stuffed figs on the prepared baking sheet, and bake for 5 to 8 minutes or until the cheese is just beginning to soften.
5. Meanwhile, toast the nuts in a dry skillet over medium heat for 2 to 5 minutes, stirring frequently to prevent burning. Toast just until fragrant, and then immediately transfer the nuts to a plate. Set aside.
6. Remove the figs from the oven, and transfer them to a serving plate using tongs. Drizzle the figs with the honey, and sprinkle on the nuts.

"*I always take figs midafternoon. They help move the bowels.*"

OLENNA TYRELL

V • YIELD: 1 CHEESECAKE; SERVES 8–10 • PREP TIME: 40 MINUTES
COOKING TIME: 45 MINUTES • DIFFICULTY: MODERATE

QUEEN OF THORNS CHEESE TART

With its rich, sweet crust and a cream and whey cheese filling, the Highgarden pastry chefs turned this simple baked cheese tart into a virtuoso dish. Delicately scented with elderflower and vanilla, and served with honey, chopped nuts, and figs, the sambocade was said to be a favorite of Lady Olenna Tyrell.

Sweet Crust (page 10) or ½ Flaky Crust (page 9)

6 large eggs, separated

¾ cup granulated sugar

1 cup cream cheese

1 cup ricotta cheese

1 teaspoon vanilla paste or extract

2 tablespoons elderflower syrup or liqueur

¼ teaspoon saffron (optional)

1 teaspoon Westerosi Sweet Spice (page 11)

¾ cup plain bread crumbs

Fresh fruit (such as fresh berries or figs), for topping (optional)

Honey, for drizzling (optional)

Chopped nuts, for topping (optional)

1. Preheat the oven to 350°F. Grease an 8-inch springform pan or a 9-inch deep-dish pie plate with butter.
2. Roll out the pie dough to a circle roughly 10 to 11 inches wide and around ⅛ inch thick. Transfer to the prepared pie tin, and gently press it into the bottoms and sides of the pan.
3. In a medium mixing bowl with a hand mixer, cream together the egg yolks and sugar until very pale. Add the cream cheese, ricotta, vanilla, elderflower syrup or liqueur, saffron, and Westerosi Sweet Spice. Beat until well blended, and then beat in the bread crumbs until well combined.
4. In a separate large mixing bowl, beat the egg whites until they are shiny and form stiff peaks. Gently fold the beaten egg whites into the cream cheese mixture.
5. Transfer the filling to the pie crust, gently smoothing it with a rubber spatula, and bake for 45 minutes until the top is golden brown and the filling in the center has set. If the filling starts to brown too much on top before the cake is fully baked, drape a sheet of aluminum foil over the cake until it's finished baking.
6. If using a springform pan, let the pie cool for 15 to 20 minutes before releasing it. Top with fresh fruit, honey, and chopped nuts.

> *The cheese will be served when I want it served. And I want it served now.*
>
> OLENNA TYRELL

V, V+*, GF* • YIELD: 4 TO 5 SERVINGS • PREP TIME: 30 MINUTES
COOKING TIME: 45 MINUTES • DIFFICULTY: MODERATE

CITADEL SOUP

Food at the Citadel, headquarters of the Order of Maesters, was basic. After all, study and scholarship were considered at odds with a rich table. Yet just as the Maesters and their young wards took their scholarship seriously, the cook and his kitchen boy took pride in their craft. Their soups and stews were artful, made from Oldtown's finest market produce. Of these, mushroom soup with cream was a favorite, although it was never remarked upon. The chef took his compliment from the cleanliness of the bowls.

- 3 ounces dried wild or porcini mushrooms
- 1 sprig rosemary
- 3 sprigs thyme
- 1 bay leaf
- 4 tablespoons butter or oil
- 3 shallots, sliced
- 6 garlic cloves, minced
- 24 ounces brown mushrooms, chopped
- ½ teaspoon salt (or to taste)
- 1 teaspoon dried marjoram
- 1 tablespoon Old Valyrian Blend (page 11)
- ¼ cup cooking sherry or Marsala wine
- 1 tablespoon Worcestershire sauce
- 5 tablespoons all-purpose flour
- 3 to 4 cups mushroom stock
- Sour cream or crème fraîche, for serving (optional)

1. Rinse the dried mushrooms to remove any grit; then soak them in 2 cups boiling water. Set aside. Using kitchen twine, tie together the rosemary, thyme, and bay leaf; set aside.
2. Heat the butter in a Dutch oven or a large, heavy-bottomed pot. Add the shallots, and sauté over medium-high heat for 2 to 3 minutes or until translucent. Add the garlic, and continue to sauté for 1 more minute until fragrant.
3. Add the fresh mushrooms, salt, marjoram, and Old Valyrian Blend. Sauté for 10 to 12 minutes, stirring occasionally, until the mushrooms brown and release their juices.
4. Add the cooking sherry or Marsala wine and the Worcestershire sauce. Continue to cook for 3 to 4 minutes until the liquid reduces significantly.
5. Reduce heat to medium-low. Sprinkle the flour over the top of the mushrooms, and continue to cook for 1 to 2 minutes. Add the mushroom stock, and whisk it in so that no lumps of flour remain. Using a wooden spoon, scrape up the browned bits in the bottom of the pan.
6. Chop up the rehydrated mushrooms, reserving both the soaking liquid and the mushrooms.
7. Add the rehydrated mushrooms and the soaking liquid to the pot, stirring well to combine. Continue to simmer for 10 minutes until the broth thickens; then add 2 to 3 cups of mushroom stock and the herb bundle. Continue to simmer for 10 to 15 minutes until the mushrooms have softened and the herbs have seeped and released flavor into the broth. You can thin out the soup with more mushroom stock until it reaches your desired soup consistency, tasting and adjusting the seasoning as necessary.
8. Serve hot in soup bowls with a side of warm bread. Top each bowl with sour cream or crème fraîche, if desired.

> “*In the Citadel, we lead different lives for different reasons. We are this world's memory, Samwell Tarly. Without us, men would be little better than dogs. Don't remember any meal but the last, can't see forward to any but the next. And every time you leave the house and shut the door, they howl like you're gone forever.*
>
> ARCHMAESTER MARWYN”

V, V+, GF • YIELD: 6 TO 8 SERVINGS • PREP TIME: 5 MINUTES
REST TIME: 2 HOURS • DIFFICULTY: EASY

ARBOR GOLD

The celebrated Arbor Gold, a potent wine likened to drinking the golden rays of the sun, is no longer made because its vines and unique terroir succumbed to the snows of winter. Many have tried to replicate its flavor by adding fruit and spices to common wine.

½ cup white grapes, sliced in half

1 pear, thinly sliced

1 apple, thinly sliced

1 cinnamon stick

1 star anise

1 bottle white wine

1 cup elderflower liqueur or cordial

1 cup apple cider

1 tablespoon orange blossom water (optional)

1. Add the grapes, pear slices, apple slices, cinnamon stick, and star anise to the bottom of a large pitcher.
2. Pour in the white wine, elderflower liqueur or cordial, apple cider, and orange blossom water, and stir. Refrigerate the mixture for at least 2 to 3 hours (ideally, overnight).
3. To serve, add some fruit slices to the glasses, and pour the infused wine over the top.

> *No more of that Dornish horse piss! This is the finest Arbor Gold. Proper wine, for proper heroes!*
>
> WALDER FREY

V • YIELD: 6 TO 12 SERVINGS • PREP TIME: 30 MINUTES
COOKING TIME: 30 MINUTES • DIFFICULTY: MODERATE

HIGHGARDEN LEMON CAKES

Lady Olenna Tyrell and her entourage always traveled with their own Highgarden chefs. It was claimed that they preferred their own superior produce and dishes, but many believed it was as much about safety as taste. At her first meeting with Sansa Stark in King's Landing, Lady Olenna had her chefs bake lemon cakes, Highgarden style, with rose water and flower petals. The light and airy sponge cakes were a gift of friendship but also a pretty bribe.

CAKE

1¼ cups all-purpose flour

¾ teaspoon baking powder

¼ teaspoon baking soda

1 to 2 tablespoons fresh lemon zest

½ teaspoon salt

½ cup unsalted butter, at room temperature

¾ cup granulated sugar

1 teaspoon vanilla extract

2 large eggs

½ cup whole milk

TOPPING

2 to 3 tablespoons lemon juice, divided

1 to 2 teaspoons rose water (optional)

1 cup confectioner's sugar

Edible flowers or flower petals, for decorating

1. Preheat the oven to 325°F. Grease ten 4-ounce ramekins or a standard muffin tin.
2. In a medium mixing bowl, whisk together the flour, baking powder, baking soda, lemon zest, and salt. Set aside.
3. Add the butter and sugar to a separate large mixing bowl, and cream together until light and fluffy, about 2 minutes. Add the vanilla and the eggs, one at a time, mixing the first egg until fully incorporated before adding the second egg.
4. Add the flour mixture in 2 to 3 additions, alternating with the milk, until fully mixed.
5. Fill the ramekins or the holes in the muffin tin about three-quarters full, and bake for 20 to 25 minutes or until a toothpick inserted into the center of one of the middle cakes comes out clean. Let the cakes cool in the tins for 5 minutes; then transfer to a cooling rack.
6. For the topping, first make the lemon glaze. Add 2 tablespoons of the lemon juice, along with the rose water and confectioner's sugar, to a small mixing bowl. Add more lemon juice as needed to thin the glaze to a pourable consistency.
7. Set a cookie sheet or some waxed paper under the wire rack where the cakes are cooling. Dip the cakes into the glaze, and then flip them upright and place them back onto the rack. Add the flowers or flower petals to the top of the cakes. Let the glaze set for 10 minutes before serving.

> *What do you say to that, Sansa? Shall we have some lemon cakes?*
>
> OLENNA TYRELL

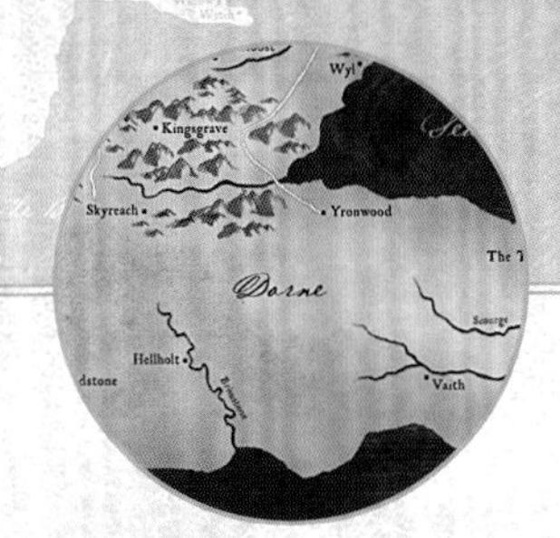

DORNE

Lush valleys and verdant oases peppered the parched sands of the southern Kingdom of Dorne. The desert land had its own distinctive cuisine, replete with citrus fruits, peppers, and spices.

The Dornish people believed their food was greater than any other regions and, when challenged, would brook no dissent.

V, V+*, GF • YIELD: 3 TO 4 SERVINGS • PREP TIME: 15 MINUTES
COOKING TIME: 5 MINUTES • DIFFICULTY: EASY

SPICED ORANGE SALAD

The orange groves of Dorne provided an abundance of sweet citrus fruit that was served fresh in salads. Blood orange wheels, pomegranate arils, finely sliced shallots, and mint were tossed with a spiced dressing to make a piquant and colorful side dish.

DRESSING

2 tablespoons lime juice

1 tablespoon olive oil

1 tablespoon honey (or to taste)

½ teaspoon orange blossom water (optional, or to taste)

1 teaspoon cinnamon

1 teaspoon Dornish Spices (page 11)

Pinch of fine salt

Harissa paste or red pepper flakes (optional, or to taste)

SALAD

¼ cup pine nuts, pistachios, or chopped pecans

6 large oranges (use a variety such as navel, Cara Cara, or blood oranges)

1 shallot, sliced very thin, divided

15 mint leaves, finely chopped, divided

¼ cup pomegranate arils

1 bird's eye chili, sliced (optional)

Crumbled goat cheese or feta (optional)

1. Optionally, toast the nuts in a dry skillet over medium heat for 2 to 5 minutes, stirring frequently to prevent burning. Toast just until fragrant; then immediately transfer the nuts to a plate and away from the skillet and heat. Set aside.
2. To make the dressing, in a small bowl, whisk together the lime juice, olive oil, honey, orange blossom water, cinnamon, Dornish Spices, salt, and harissa paste or red pepper flakes. Set aside.
3. Peel the oranges, removing as much of the pith as possible from the flesh. Slice the oranges into wheels.
4. Drizzle a third of the dressing all around the serving plate, and sprinkle on half the shallots and mint. Arrange the orange wheels on the serving plate over the dressing/shallot layer. Drizzle with the remaining dressing. Sprinkle on the remaining mint and shallots, along with the pomegranate arils, nuts, sliced chilis to taste, and goat cheese or feta. Serve immediately.

> *I have deep knowledge of the port at Sunspear, where I've seen the ships of Essos setting sail with their hulls full of oranges and cinnamon, and I've always wished to see where they went.*
>
> CRISTON COLE

LEMON AND GOAT CHEESE DIP

This flavorful dip made from goat cheese and cream was enriched with Dornish spices and served with purple olives, hot pepper sauce, and olive oil. Small dishes were presented on trays with grilled vegetables and warmed flat bread.

DIP

4 ounces soft goat cheese, at room temperature

½ cup labneh, plain Greek yogurt, or sour cream

1 to 2 tablespoons lemon zest

2 tablespoons lemon juice

1 to 2 teaspoons Dornish Spices (page 11)

Salt

Black pepper

1 large garlic clove, minced

¼ cup chopped fresh herbs (such as parsley, mint, or cilantro), plus more for garnish

Kalamata olives, pitted and halved

Harissa paste or other hot pepper sauce, for serving (optional)

Extra virgin olive oil, for serving

SUGGESTED ACCOMPANIMENTS

Flat bread, such as pita or naan

Grilled vegetables

Sliced cucumbers

Sliced bell peppers or mini sweet peppers

Sliced radishes

Figs and dates

Assorted olives

1. In a small mixing bowl, whip together the goat cheese; labneh, Greek yogurt, or sour cream; lemon zest; lemon juice; Dornish spices, salt, and pepper; garlic; and fresh herbs. This can be done by hand or with a hand mixer. Taste, and adjust seasoning as needed.
2. Spoon the mixture into a container with a lid, and refrigerate for at least 1 hour (up to overnight).
3. Let the mixture come to room temperature, and then spoon it into a shallow bowl for serving.
4. Top with olives, harissa paste, a generous drizzle of olive oil, and additional chopped herbs.
5. Serve with an assortment of dippers.

V • YIELD: 8 SERVINGS • PREP TIME: 45 MINUTES
COOKING TIME: 1 HOUR • DIFFICULTY: MODERATE

DORNISH CHEESE AND PEPPER PIE

Creamy pungent brined cheese and peppers were key cook's ingredients in Dorne and were often combined in a pie. Crisp, paper-thin pastry sheets encased the liquescent cheese; the whole dish topped with sesame seeds and pitted olives.

¾ cup ricotta cheese

2 tablespoons extra virgin olive oil, plus more for brushing

1 medium onion, finely chopped

6 green onions, sliced

6 garlic cloves, minced

2 red bell peppers, sliced

1 orange bell pepper, sliced

1 yellow bell pepper, sliced

1 green bell pepper, sliced

1½ cups crumbled feta cheese

2 tablespoons fresh dill or 2 to 3 teaspoons dried dill

2 teaspoons Dornish Spices (page 11)

1 teaspoon lemon zest

1 teaspoon red pepper flakes (optional)

Salt

Black pepper

2 large eggs, lightly beaten

1 package phyllo dough, thawed

¼ cup pitted Kalamata or Castelvetrano olives, plus more for garnish

Sesame seeds, for garnish

1. Line a fine-mesh strainer with cheesecloth and place it over a bowl. Add the ricotta to the strainer and cover with plastic wrap, then place a heavy object (such as a plate) on top. Transfer to the refrigerator and let it drain for at least 4 hours or overnight.
2. Preheat the oven to 350°F. Grease a 9-inch pie plate or small cast iron skillet.
3. Heat 1 tablespoon olive oil in a large skillet over medium high heat. Add the onion, and cook until soft and lightly browned, about 5 minutes. Add the green onions and garlic, and cook for another minute.
4. Add more oil, if necessary, and then add the bell peppers. Continue to cook on medium hight heat until the peppers have softened and browned somewhat, about 6 to 8 minutes. Remove from heat, and set aside to cool.
5. To a large mixing bowl, add the ricotta, feta, dill, Dornish Spices, lemon zest, red pepper flakes, and salt and pepper to taste. When the pepper mixture is no longer hot, add it to the mixing bowl, and stir everything together until well combined. Taste, and adjust seasonings to your liking; then stir in the eggs.
6. Layer 6 sheets of filo dough in the pan, brushing each with olive oil before adding the next layer, and rotating each sheet so the corners are pointing different directions.
7. Add the cheese and pepper mixture, and use a rubber spatula to spread it out evenly. Sprinkle or arrange the olives on top of the cheese and pepper mixture.

Continued on page 154

"*The pie looks good.*

BRONN"

8. Cover with 6 oil-brushed phyllo sheets, using the same criss-cross method in step 5. Roll in the excess phyllo to create a border. Brush the top with oil, and create slits with a knife to vent steam. Sprinkle sesame seeds over the top.
9. Bake on the middle rack for 35 to 45 minutes or until the pastry is golden and crispy. Check periodically to make sure the pie is not becoming too dark on top. If becoming too dark on top, loosely cover the top with aluminum foil for the remainder of the baking time. Garnish with olives, and let cool for 15 minutes before slicing and serving.

GRILLED PEACHES

Sweet peaches were dusted with toasted nuts and spices, and then grilled and served with soft white cheese and honey. The Dornish speciality was often eaten beneath the arbors at Sunspear before sundown.

- Chopped pistachios or pecans
- 4 ripe but firm peaches, halved and pitted
- 1 tablespoon extra virgin olive oil
- ½ teaspoon ground cinnamon (or to taste)
- ¼ teaspoon ground cardamom (or to taste, optional)
- 1 cup labneh or plain full-fat Greek yogurt
- Seeds of 1 vanilla bean
- 2 teaspoons honey, plus more for drizzling
- Fresh mint, chopped, for garnish

1. Optionally, toast the nuts in a dry skillet over medium heat for 2 to 5 minutes, stirring frequently to prevent burning. Toast just until fragrant; then immediately remove from the skillet, and heat. Set aside.
2. Brush the peaches with the oil. Sprinkle on the cinnamon and cardamom.
3. Heat a grill pan over medium heat. Place the peaches on the grill, cut side down, and cook until grill marks appear, about 4 to 5 minutes. Flip the peaches over, and cook them for another 3 to 4 minutes on the second side.
4. Meanwhile, whisk together the labneh or yogurt, vanilla seeds, and honey in a small bowl until well combined. Taste, and adjust sweetness as desired.
5. When the peaches are done, place them on the serving plate. Add a generous dollop of the labneh or yogurt on each. Drizzle with honey, and sprinkle with nuts and fresh mint.

> *The Dornishman's wife would sing as she bathed, in a voice that was sweet as a peach . . .*
>
> BRONN

V, V+, GF • YIELD: 6 TO 8 SERVINGS • PREP TIME: 30 MINUTES
COOKING TIME: 90 MINUTES • DIFFICULTY: MODERATE

SUNSPEAR SOUP

The Dornish capital was a center for fine cuisine, but a simple spiced soup assumed the city's name. Made with red lentils carried by ships from Essos, the soup is flavored with onion, garlic, turmeric, and Dornish spices, with herbs, lemons, and red pepper flakes to taste. It was said to promote vigor and was eaten by the infirm and would-be warriors alike, both of whom swore by its virtue and exquisite piquancy.

1½ cups dried red lentils

1 to 2 tablespoons olive oil

1 large yellow onion, diced

4 garlic cloves, minced

1 teaspoon ground turmeric

1 tablespoon Dornish Spices (page 11)

Fine salt

2 medium carrots, chopped

2 ribs celery, chopped

8 to 10 cups chicken or vegetable stock, divided

1 medium potato, peeled and roughly diced

⅓ cup cilantro or flat-leaf parsley, chopped, plus more for serving

2 to 3 tablespoons lemon juice (or to taste)

1 teaspoon lemon zest

Red pepper flakes (optional)

Bird's eye chile, thinly sliced, for serving (optional)

Lemon slices, for serving

1. Rinse the lentils until the water runs almost clear; set aside.
2. Heat the oil in a Dutch oven or a medium skillet over medium-high heat. Add the onion, and sauté for 2 minutes until fragrant. Add the garlic, turmeric, Dornish Spices, and salt to taste; continue to sauté for 2 to 3 more minutes. Add the carrots, and sauté until they have softened somewhat, about 3 to 4 minutes. Add the celery, and sauté for another 2 minutes.
3. To a large soup or stock pot, add 8 cups of the broth, along with the lentils, the potato, and the veggies from the skillet. Bring to a boil over high heat; then reduce heat to low, and cover. Simmer over low heat for at least 45 to 60 minutes until the lentils have softened completely. Check, and stir occasionally to prevent burning on the bottom.
4. Blend the soup with a hand blender, or transfer it in batches to a regular blender. If you are using a regular blender, let the soup cool a bit before you blend, to avoid building up too much pressure from the heat. The safest approach is to blend the soup in batches so your blender is never more than three-quarters full. Blend for 1 to 2 minutes until the soup is completely smooth and creamy. Alternatively, use a potato masher or ricer to blend the soup, but this will take some time and effort.
5. Return the soup to the pot. Add the cilantro or parsley, and simmer on low for another 10 to 15 minutes, stirring occasionally to prevent any burning on the bottom.
6. Remove from heat, and stir in the lemon juice, lemon zest, and red pepper flakes. Taste, and adjust seasoning as desired. Add more broth for a thinner consistency, if desired.
7. Ladle into serving bowls, garnished with additional parsley or cilantro, sliced bird's eye chile, and lemon slices. Serve hot.

V, V+*, GF • YIELD: 4 SERVINGS • PREP TIME: 20 MINUTES
COOKING TIME: W • DIFFICULTY: EASY

CANDIED PLUMS

Plump, crystalline sugar plum spheres spiced with a hint of rum were a Dornish delicacy. The candied sweets were a celebration treat, gifted by travelers from the south to friends and acquaintances across Westeros. They were also used as bribes, and many a child was persuaded to spill a secret in exchange for the pretty confections.

1 cup chopped nuts (choose your favorites)

1 cup dried plums (prunes)

⅔ cup whole dates, pitted

3 tablespoons spiced rum (or to taste)

1 teaspoon honey

1 teaspoon orange zest

1 teaspoon vanilla extract

¼ teaspoon fine salt

2 teaspoons cinnamon

½ teaspoon ground allspice

½ teaspoon ground ginger

¼ teaspoon ground cardamom

½ cup plum or purple-colored sanding sugar

Rosemary leaves (optional, for decor)

1. Add all the ingredients except the granulated sugar to a food processor. Pulse just until everything starts to stick together in a large ball.
2. Remove the ball from the processor, and form the mixture into small plum-like ovals about 1 inch in diameter.
3. Roll each ball in colored sanding sugar, to coat. Garnish each with 1 to 2 rosemary leaves.
4. Roll each oval in colored sanding sugar, to coat. Use a skewer or the side of a fork to make a small indentation in each oval. Garnish each with 1 to 2 rosemary leaves
5. Serve immediately or store in an airtight container in the refrigerator for up to 2 weeks

> *It's funny you should mention that. Guess what I happened to find today. Candied plums from Dorne.*
>
> QYBURN

DORNISH RED

Dornish red was not for the fragile. An intense wine with citrus notes and a spiced aroma, the tart liquor had a spicy kick that pleased southern natives and surprised outsiders, who were urged to drink with caution.

½ hot chile pepper, sliced (optional)

2 to 3 ounces dark red wine, such as Syrah

2 ounces tequila

1 ounce orange liqueur

1 ounce lime juice

½ ounce agave syrup

1 star anise or blood orange wheel, for garnish (optional)

1. In a cocktail shaker, lightly muddle the hot chile pepper.
2. Fill the cocktail shaker with ice.
3. Add the remaining ingredients.
4. Shake vigorously for 10 to 15 seconds.
5. Strain into the serving glass.
6. Garnish with a star anise or a blood orange slice.

> *How can you drink this piss? When we reach Sunspear, I'll treat you to a Dornish red, the best in the world. Have you ever been to Dorne?*
>
> ELLARIA SAND

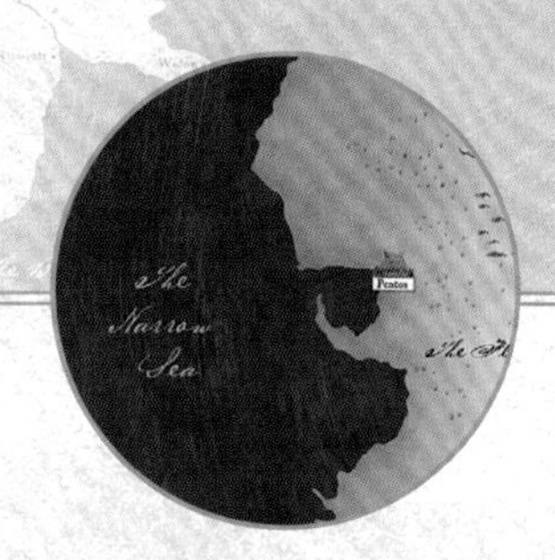

ACROSS THE NARROW SEA

To the east of Westeros lies the vast continent of Essos—a land of forest, mountain, rugged gorges, desert, and steppe. Wealthy cities lined its coasts, from Braavos in the north to Qarth in the east. Trade supplied every luxury that could be shipped for gold. The continent's cuisine was as varied as its people, and its drink had such potency that it was rumored to come from the realms of magic.

GF • YIELD: 2 TO 4 SERVINGS • PREP TIME: 20 MINUTES
REST TIME: 2 HOURS • COOKING TIME: 40 MINUTES • DIFFICULTY: MODERATE

ROASTED LAMB

Sheep were both a staple and a delicacy in Essos. They were raised in the hills by smallfolk, who drank their milk and made cheese, although could rarely afford to eat their valuable meat. After slaughter, the mutton and lamb went to the tables of the wealthy. From head to heart, no part was wasted, and each was the subject of cultural—and personal—preference.

The princes of Pentos preferred rack of lamb, expertly seasoned, marinated, and roasted in their vast kitchen ovens, and served on Rizmon Mālor with an herb sauce. This dish was a known favorite of Reggio Haratis, ruler of the free city during the War for the Stepstones; his cooks made fragrant and tender cuts from this primal rib.

1 rack of lamb (about 2 pounds), trimmed

1 to 2 teaspoons fine salt

½ teaspoon black pepper

1 to 2 teaspoons Essosi Spices (page 12)

10 garlic cloves

1 large shallot, quartered

½ cup fresh herbs (such as mint, parsley, rosemary, and cilantro), chopped

2 teaspoons dried oregano

¼ cup olive oil, plus 2 tablespoons for searing

2 tablespoons lemon juice

1 tablespoon pomegranate molasses or honey

¼ cup ground raw pistachios or panko bread crumbs (optional)

PAIRS WELL WITH:

Meereenese Herb Sauce (page 15)

Rizmon Mālor (page 167)

1. Season the lamb with the salt, pepper, and Essosi Spices; set aside.
2. To a blender, add the garlic, shallot, fresh herbs, oregano, ¼ cup olive oil, lemon juice, and pomegranate molasses or honey. Purée until it forms a paste. Rub the mixture all over the lamb, working it into the slits.
3. Wrap the lamb in plastic wrap, and place it into a container (to catch leaks). Allow it to marinate at room temperature for about 2 hours. Then remove the plastic wrap, but allow whatever marinade sticks to the lamb to stay there. You can also marinate the lamb overnight in the refrigerator, but make sure the lamb comes to room temperature before roasting, about 60 to 90 minutes.
4. Preheat the oven to 450°F. Line a baking sheet with parchment paper, and place the lamb on top, bone side down. Sprinkle on the ground pistachios or panko, if using, lightly pressing them into the lamb with your hands to adhere them. Cover loosely with aluminum foil.
5. Roast the lamb on the upper rack of the oven for 15 minutes, and then remove the foil. Roast for another 15 to 20 minutes until the lamb is nicely browned and an instant-read thermometer inserted in the center reads at least 135°F (for medium rare) or up to 145°F (for medium well). Let rest for 15 minutes before serving on a bed of Rizmon Mālor with a side of Meereenese Herb Sauce, if desired.

RIZMON MĀLOR (SAND RICE)

This golden spiced wheat dish was known in High Valyrian as Rizmon Mālor, or "sand rice," for its resemblance to the shifting sands of Essos.

Although its raw ingredients were cheap, the dish was greater than the sum of its parts, and the skillfully seasoned couscous graced many Free City banquets.

⅓ cup pine nuts

2 tablespoons unsalted butter

1 shallot, chopped

3 garlic cloves, minced

2 teaspoons Essosi Spices (page 12)

½ teaspoon saffron threads (optional)

Salt

Black pepper

2 cups chicken or vegetable broth

1 cup ultrafine couscous

½ cup sultanas (golden raisins)

⅓ cup chopped fresh cilantro or flat-leaf parsley

2 tablespoons lemon juice

1 tablespoon olive oil

1. Toast the pine nuts in a dry skillet over medium heat for 3 to 5 minutes, stirring frequently to prevent burning. Toast until fragrant and lightly browned; then immediately remove the skillet from heat. Set aside.
2. Melt the butter in a Dutch oven or a large saucepan over medium-high heat. Add the shallot, garlic, Essosi Spices, saffron, and salt and pepper to taste. Sauté until the onions are translucent, stirring occasionally, about 4 to 5 minutes.
3. Pour the broth into the pot. Increase heat to medium-high, and bring to a boil. As soon as the liquid begins to boil, remove the pan from heat. Stir in the couscous, cover, and let sit for 10 minutes.
4. Fluff up the couscous with a fork. Add the sultanas, cilantro or parsley, lemon juice, olive oil, and toasted nuts to the pot. Stir together the ingredients. Taste, and adjust seasoning as needed. Serve hot.

GF • YIELD: 2 TO 4 SERVINGS • PREP TIME: 30 MINUTES
COOKING TIME: 25 MINUTES • REST TIME: 10 MINUTES • DIFFICULTY: MODERATE

DROGON'S FLAME-GRILLED FISH

Dragons ate no food raw. Daenerys Targaryen's dragons seared their own meat and fish, catching, tossing, flaming, and swallowing them fresh from land and sea.

Seasoned fish from Slaver's Bay was cooked similarly by its citizens, flavored with leeks and garlic and then seared on an oiled grill.

1 whole fish (such as branzino, sea bass, or trout), cleaned and gutted (about 1 pound)

1 tablespoon Old Valyrian Blend (page 11)

1 to 2 teaspoons fine salt (or to taste)

½ teaspoon black pepper (or to taste)

2 garlic cloves, minced, divided

1 leek, white and light green parts only, sliced into rounds about ⅛ inch thick

¼ cup fresh herbs (such as parsley, dill, or basil), chopped

1 lemon, sliced

4 to 6 toothpicks, soaked in water

1 green onion, chopped

2 tablespoons olive oil, plus more for greasing

Meereenese Herb Sauce (page 15), for serving (optional)

1. Dry the fish with paper towels. Use a sharp knife to cut 3 to 4 slits on each side of the fish.
2. Season the fish all over with the Old Valyrian Blend, salt, and pepper, paying extra attention to the inside of the cavity.
3. Rub three-quarters of the minced garlic on the inside of the cavity. Stuff the cavity with the leek, herbs, and lemon slices. Use the soaked toothpicks to seal the cavity shut.
4. Stuff the slits you made earlier with the remaining garlic and the green onions.
5. Drizzle the 2 tablespoons of olive oil all around the fish on both sides.
6. Brush the grate of your grill with oil. Bring the grill to 400°F. Grill the fish in direct heat until lightly charred, about 10 to 12 minutes. Don't try to move the fish before then; it will stick to the grates. Flip the fish over, and grill on the other side until cooked throughout, about 10 minutes more.
7. Transfer the fish to a serving platter, and let rest for 10 minutes. Serve with Meereenese Herb Sauce (page 15), and drizzle with a little more olive oil, if desired.

GF • YIELD: 4 TO 6 SERVINGS • PREP TIME: 30 MINUTES • REST TIME: 2 HOURS
COOKING TIME: 3–4 HOURS (MOSTLY IDLE) • DIFFICULTY: MODERATE

KHALEESI'S SUPPER

The Dothraki staple food was horseflesh, but the nomads raided or traded meat, grasses, spices, and rice with the people of the Essosi steppes. Live goats were bartered and butchered, and the fresh meat was coated and left to stand in a fiery mix of continental spices. Cuts were cooked in a heavy pot over an open fire, simmered in a broth of fragrant grasses and pepper pods, and served with wild rice.

2 to 3 pounds goat meat (or use lamb stew meat or oxtails)

12 garlic cloves, minced, divided

2 tablespoons minced fresh ginger, divided

1 to 2 teaspoons fine salt

4 tablespoons curry powder, divided

4 tablespoons Essosi Spices (page 12), divided

2 to 4 tablespoons oil, divided, plus more as needed

4 shallots, chopped

1 ghost pepper or other hot pepper, chopped (optional)

6 stalks lemongrass, tender insides only, minced

5 bay leaves

2 to 4 cups chicken broth, divided

1 to 2 tablespoons honey

Cooked wild rice, for serving (optional)

1. In a medium mixing bowl, coat the meat with half the minced garlic, half the minced ginger, the salt, half the curry powder, half the Essosi Spices, and 1 to 2 tablespoons of the oil. Cover the bowl, and let it sit at room temperature for at least 2 hours, or chill in the refrigerator for up to 12 hours.
2. Heat the remaining oil in a large Dutch oven or other heavy pot over medium-high heat. Working in batches, add the goat (no need to remove any marinade) and cook, turning occasionally, until the outside is lightly cooked and the marinade darkens in color, about 2 minutes per side. Transfer the meat to a plate, and set aside.
3. To the same pot the meat was cooked in, add the shallots, the rest of the garlic, the chopped hot pepper, the lemongrass, and the remaining spices. Cook, stirring and scraping up any browned bits stuck to the bottom of the pot, for 4 to 5 minutes until softened.
4. Return the meat to the pot, along with any remaining marinade. Add the bay leaves and 2 cups of chicken broth. Gently stir to combine.
5. Bring to a boil over medium-high heat; then reduce the temperature to low. Partially cover the pot, and continue to simmer, stirring gently every 15 to 20 minutes. The liquid will evaporate completely after a while: When this happens, add just enough broth to scrape up the browned bits stuck to the bottom of the pot. Repeat this process of simmering and adding broth until the meat is falling from the bone and the curry is thick and deeply browned, about 2 to 3 hours total. Stir in the honey just before serving.
6. Serve hot over cooked wild rice.

"*I'll have the boys butcher a goat for supper.*

JORAH MORMONT"

V, V+*, GF • YIELD: 1 SERVING • PREP TIME: 15 MINUTES
COOKING TIME: 15 MINUTES • DIFFICULTY: EASY

TYROSHI PEAR BRANDY

The Free City of Tyrosh, at the eastern end of the Stepstones, was known for its pear brandy. This fragrant distilled wine drink, with notes of vanilla, cinnamon, and ginger, was highly prized and shipped to cities east and west.

SPICED SYRUP

¼ cup water

¼ cup honey

1 to 2 cinnamon sticks

1 to 2 star anise

2-inch piece of fresh ginger, chopped

1 teaspoon vanilla extract

DRINK

2 ounces brandy

½ ounce lemon juice

¾ ounce Spiced Syrup

2 ounces pear juice or pear nectar

Pear slice, for garnish (optional)

Star anise, for garnish (optional)

1. Add the water, honey, cinnamon sticks, star anise, and chopped ginger to a small saucepan. Bring to a simmer over medium heat, stirring until the honey dissolves. Reduce heat to low, and simmer for 5 to 6 minutes. Take the syrup off the heat, stir in the vanilla, and allow it to cool and steep for 10 to 15 minutes.
2. Strain the syrup through a fine mesh strainer into a heatproof storage container with a lid, such as a mason jar. Discard the solids. Refrigerate until chilled and ready to use.
3. To make the drink, add the brandy, lemon juice, Spiced Syrup, and pear juice or nectar into a cocktail shaker filled with ice.
4. Shake for 10 to 15 seconds until well chilled.
5. Strain into a serving glass, and garnish with a pear slice and a star anise.

> *Virzetha ğizikhven! Mra qora! Mra qora! Sweet reds! I have sweet reds from Lys, Volantis, and the Arbor! Tyrosh pear brandy! Andalish sours! I have them! I have them!*
>
> WINE MERCHANT

V, V+, GF • YIELD: 1 SERVING • PREP TIME: 5 MINUTES • DIFFICULTY: EASY

SHADE OF THE EVENING

The House of the Undying, headquarters of the Warlocks of Qarth, was subject to one of the magicians' many magical deceptions. It was a round tower with no doors, yet somehow—it was reported—one found oneself inside.

The warlocks within drank a potion known as Shade of the Evening that stained their lips blue; in this potion, their power was said to reside. Recipes echo the flavor of that drink, but the magic—if indeed there was magic, not just trickery—has long since dissipated.

2 ounces gin

1 ounce blue curaçao

½ ounce lime juice

½ ounce anise liqueur*

¾ ounce orgeat (or simple syrup with almond extract)

Pinch of white edible luster dust (optional)

2 to 3 ounces tonic water or club soda, chilled

1 small piece dry ice (optional)

1. Add the gin, blue curaçao, lime juice, anisette, orgeat, and luster dust to a cocktail shaker filled with ice.
2. Shake for 10 to 15 seconds until well chilled.
3. Strain into the serving glass, and top off with tonic water.
4. Use a pair of tongs to drop a small piece of dry ice into the drink, being extremely careful not to touch it. Wait until the ice fully dissipates before taking a sip.

If you don't like the flavor of licorice, use almond liqueur.

It is where the warlocks go to squint at dusty books and drink shade of the evening. It turns their lips blue and their minds soft. So soft, they actually believe their parlor tricks are magic.

XARO XHOAN DAXOS

V, V+*, GF • YIELD: 1 SERVING • PREP TIME: 5 MINUTES
COOKING TIME: 15 MINUTES • DIFFICULTY: EASY

DUSK ROSE TEA

The warm infusion known as dusk rose tea was widely drunk in Essos to ease a fever. The floral, honey-sweetened tea was said to resemble the purple rose tinged twilight skies of Slaver's Bay.

1 tablespoon dried butterfly pea flowers

2 teaspoons dried chamomile flowers

2 teaspoons dried rosebud tea or ½ teaspoon rose water

2 to 4 whole allspice berries, lightly crushed

1 cup almost boiling water (190° to 195°F)

2 teaspoons honey (or to taste)

1 tablespoon lemon juice

1. In a heat-resistant glass, such as a mug, add the dried flowers and allspice berries. Pour the hot water over the flowers, and let steep for 8 to 10 minutes.
2. Strain the tea through a fine mesh strainer into a serving cup, such as a glass mug. If using rose water, add it now.
3. Stir in the honey, and then add the lemon juice to taste. The tea will change color when the lemon juice is added.

> *You have to know a land to rule it. Its plants, its rivers, its roads, its people. Dusk rose tea eases fever. Everyone in Meereen knows that. Especially the slaves who have to make the tea. If you want them to follow you, you have to become a part of their world.*
>
> DAARIO NAHARIS

GF • YIELD: 2 TO 3 SERVINGS • PREP TIME: 30 MINUTES
REST TIME: 1 HOUR • COOKING TIME: 0–12 MINUTES • DIFFICULTY: MODERATE

A GIRL'S OYSTERS WITH VINEGAR

The oysters of Braavos were a wonder from Essos. Served from quayside barrows with an herb and vinegar sauce, they were shucked and swallowed straight from the shell.

½ cup white wine vinegar

1 small shallot, minced

¼ teaspoon salt

½ teaspoon cracked black pepper

½ teaspoon honey

2 tablespoons chopped fresh herbs (such as cilantro, parsley, chives, and tarragon)

1 dozen raw oysters

1. Add the vinegar, shallot, salt, pepper, honey, and herbs in a small mixing bowl, and then whisk to combine. Set aside at room temperature for at least 1 hour (or in the fridge overnight). You may want to prepare the sauce before you even buy the oysters.
2. Shuck the oysters carefully. It's best to do this over a bowl, to catch any liquid (or "liquor") that might spill; this liquid is a crucial part of the oyster's flavor. If you're not cooking the oysters and you see any oysters already open, toss them—they are no longer safe to eat raw. Set one of the oysters on a dish towel, rounded side down, and insert a sharp knife into the hinge. Pull the knife down and then across, and cut the muscle.
3. When the oyster is open, it should smell salty and briny, like the sea. If it smells fishy, it is likely no longer safe to eat. Remove any grit, sand, or bits of shell inside, but try not to spill the liquor. Repeat this process for all the oysters. When done, add the spilled liquor in the bowl back to the bottom shells with the oyster meat.
4. Preheat the grill to high, or preheat the oven to 400°F.
5. Lay the oysters on the grill, and grill until the liquid just begins to simmer but the oysters are still a little raw in the center, about 4 to 5 minutes. Using tongs, carefully remove the oysters from the grill. If using an oven, broil the oysters on a baking sheet on the top rack for 8 to 12 minutes.

Continued on page 180

> *Very nice. Give me four. With vinegar.*
>
> THIN MAN

6. Add the vinegar mixture to a small shallow bowl, and place the bowl in the center of the plate. Arrange the oysters around the sauce on the plate. Serve immediately.
7. To eat, use a small fork to detach the oyster from the shell; then spoon some of the vinegar sauce onto the oyster. Pick up the shell, and slurp the oyster along with the vinegar and shallots from the wide end of the shell.

NOTE: *If you're a fan of raw seafood, skip cooking the oysters. After shucking the oysters, cover a rimmed plate with crushed ice; arrange the shucked raw oysters on top, making sure not to spill any of the oyster's liquor. Keep the center of the plate free for the vinegar sauce, and arrange the oysters around it.*

V • YIELD: 8 TO 10 SERVINGS • PREP TIME: 30 MINUTES
COOKING TIME: 45 MINUTES • DIFFICULTY: MODERATE

PLUM CAKE

Caramelized plum cake was a Pentos delight. The lightly spiced cake was baked with butter, sugar, and rum-doused plums at the pan base, and then for serving so the sticky glazed plums sat on top.

TOPPING

¼ cup unsalted butter, melted

1 tablespoon spiced rum

⅓ cup light brown sugar

6 plums, pitted and sliced ¼ inch thick

CAKE

1½ cups all-purpose flour

¾ teaspoon baking soda

1½ teaspoons ground cinnamon

1 teaspoon ground allspice

¾ teaspoon ground ginger

¼ teaspoon ground cardamom (optional)

¾ teaspoon fine salt

¾ cup unsalted butter, softened

½ cup dark brown sugar

2 eggs

¾ cup full-fat plain Greek yogurt

1 teaspoon vanilla paste or extract

1. Preheat the oven to 375°F. Grease a 9-inch round cake pan.
2. Add the melted butter and rum to the cake pan. Add the light brown sugar to the pan, and spread it so that it evenly covers the bottom of the pan.
3. Arrange the plum slices in concentric circles, overlapping slightly, working from the outer edges to the center. Set aside the pan.
4. In a medium mixing bowl, whisk together the flour, baking soda, spices, and salt. Set aside.
5. In a large mixing bowl with a hand mixer, or in the bowl of a stand mixer, add the softened butter and brown sugar. Beat on medium-high speed for 3 minutes or until the mixture is fluffy.
6. Add in the eggs, and beat until blended. Add the yogurt and vanilla. Beat until the mixture is smooth, scraping the sides of the bowl with a rubber spatula as needed.
7. Reduce the mixer speed to low, and slowly incorporate the flour mixture into the butter mixture, just until fully incorporated. Try not to overmix.
8. Spoon the cake batter into the pan with the plums, spreading it evenly over the plum layer and smoothing it with a rubber spatula.
9. Bake for 40 to 45 minutes or until a toothpick inserted in the center of the cake comes out clean.
10. Cool the cake for 10 to 15 minutes. Run a knife along the side of the pan, to release it. Place a flat serving plate over the cake pan, and carefully flip the cake upside down onto the plate.
11. Serve the cake warm or at room temperature.

> “*There's a plum cake yet to be served, which will have us fighting over the crumbs.*”
>
> LAENA VELARYON

THE WESTEROSI TABLE

SUBSTITUTIONS

Not all ingredients used in the historic span of this book are available today—and those that are might not be to the taste of today's cooks. The following substitutions can be used for alcohol, dairy and eggs, meat, honey, flour, and sugar.

ALCOHOL

NOTE: *When cooking alcohol, most of the alcohol will cook off; the little that remains in the finished dish will not have any intoxicating effect.*

RED WINE

In drinks and desserts:

- Non-alcoholic red wine
- Pomegranate Juice (page 51)

In soups, stews, and pie fillings:

- Non-alcoholic red wine
- 2:1 combination of beef broth and red wine vinegar

WHITE WINE

In drinks and desserts:

- Non-alcoholic white wine
- Apple juice
- White grape juice

In soups, stews, and pie fillings:

- Non-alcoholic white wine
- 2:1 combination of chicken broth and white wine vinegar

BEER AND ALE

In bread/baking:

- Dark beer: Non-alcoholic dark beer, Kvass, or Cola
- Light beer: Non-alcoholic light beer, ginger ale, or Club Soda

In soups, stews, and pie fillings:

- Dark beer: Non-alcoholic dark beer or 2:1 beef broth plus balsamic vinegar
- Light beer: Non-alcoholic light beer or 2:1 chicken broth plus malt vinegar

OTHER LIQUORS

- Rum: Spiced apple cider plus a few drops of rum extract
- Brandy: 2:1 apple juice and lemon juice plus a few drops of brandy extract (optional)
- Mead: 1:1 pulp-free orange juice and honey syrup
- Cooking wines: 1:1 apple juice and broth
- Orange liqueur: Orange juice
- Equivalent commercial substitutes
- Sparkling water (for light or clear liquors)
- Ginger ale (for medium liquors)
- Sparkling apple juice (for darker liquors)

DAIRY AND EGGS

EGGS

For baked goods:

- Commercial egg substitute
- ¼ cup unsweetened apple sauce, mashed pumpkin, or puréed fruit plus ½ teaspoon baking powder (per 1 egg)

For binding:

- Commercial egg substitute
- 3 tablespoons water plus 1 tablespoon flax seeds or chia seeds

For custards:

- 1 tablespoon custard powder or cornstarch mixed with 2 tablespoons water

MILK

- Full-fat non-dairy milk, such as a nut milk or oat milk

CREAM

- Generally: Full-fat nondairy cream
- For whipping: Full-fat coconut cream

BUTTER

- Plant butter
- Coconut oil
- Margarine
- Shortening

MEATS

Red Meat

- Commercial beef substitutes
- Mushrooms
- Tempeh
- Seitan
- Jackfruit

White Meat

- Commercial chicken substitutes
- Soy curls
- Seitan
- Tempeh
- Jackfruit

Bacon

- Vegan: Commercial vegan bacon substitute
- Kosher or halal: Turkey or duck bacon

Pork

- Commercial pork substitute
- Jackfruit
- Seitan
- Soy curls

Ground Meat

- Commercial ground meat substitutes
- Textured soy protein
- Lentils (1 cup uncooked lentils – 1 pound ground meat)
- Crumbled extra-firm tofu

Fish

- Commercial fish substitutes
- Jackfruit
- Lion's mane mushrooms
- Cooked eggplant

Broth

- For beef broth:
  - Mushroom stock
- For chicken broth:
  - Vegetable broth

** When substituting meat products, note that cooking times may vary. For most soups, stews, and pie fillings, cooking times will be shortened.*

OTHER

Honey

- Golden syrup
- Maple syrup
- Regular molasses (not blackstrap)

All-Purpose Flour

- Almond flour
- Coconut flour

Granulated Sugar

- Commercial sugar substitutes
- Cane sugar
- Palm sugar

Brown Sugar

- Commercial brown sugar substitutes
- 1:1 granulated sugar or sugar alternative plus 1 tablespoon molasses

HOT PIE'S DIREWOLF BREAD TEMPLATE

Top this image with a sheet of clean paper. Trace the template with a pencil or edible ink marker. Take the sheet of paper with the direwolf traced on it and cut out the outline using a scissors. Place the paper stencil onto the rolled dough. Use a sharp knife to cut the direwolf shape into the rolled dough, using the paper stencil as a guide. Alternatively, work freehand to cut and shape the direwolves using this image as a reference (results may vary).

DIETARY CONSIDERATIONS

V: Vegetarian • V+: Vegan GF: Gluten-free • V*: Easily adapted to be vegetarian
V+*: Easily adapted to be vegan • GF*: Easily adapted to be gluten-free

THE CROWNLANDS	V	V+	GF	V*	V+*	GF*
Princeling's Porridge	X					
Rhaenyra's Lemon Cakes	X					
Stuffed "Dragon" Eggs	X					
Poached Pears	X		X		X	
Larys Strong's Meat Pie						
Roast Duck			X			
Honeyed Game Birds			X			
Milk of the Poppy	X		X		X	
Roasted Boar			X			
Burnt Lemon Tarts	X					
Shae's Fish Pie						
Mulled Wine	X	X	X			
Pigeon Pie						
Lamprey Pie						
Iced Milk	X		X		X	
Bowl of Brown						X
Pomegranate Juice	X	X	X			

THE NORTH & BEYOND THE WALL	V	V+	GF	V*	V+*	GF*
Hobb's Venison Stew with Onions						X
Rat Cook's Pie						
Pork Chops and Apples			X			
Armored Turnips	X		X			
Ramsey Snow's Pork Sausage						X
Winterfell Bread Pudding	X					
Mance Rayder's Proper Northern Drink	X		X			
Walnut Pie	X					
Meat and Mead			X			
Breakfast of the North						
Giant's Milk	X		X			
Roasted Potatoes			X	X	X	
Hot Spiced Cider	X	X	X			

THE RIVERLANDS & THE VALE OF ARRYN	V	V+	GF	V*	V+*	GF*
Mutton Stew						
Hot Pie's Sour Cherry Tarts	X					
Brown Bread	X				X	
Hot Pie's Direwolf Bread	X					
Thoros's Blackstrap Rum	X	X	X			
Guest Rites (Bread and Salt)	X					
The Hound's Whole Chicken			X			
Rabbit Stew						X
Candied Almonds	X		X		X	
Honey Cakes	X					
Moon Custard	X					
Kidney Pie						
Eyrie Lemon Cakes	X					
Minced Frey Pie						

THE WESTERLANDS & THE IRON ISLANDS	V	V+	GF	V*	V+*	GF*
Honeyed Wine	X		X			
Turtle Stew						X
Gingerbread Castles	X					
Iron Islands Grog	X	X	X			
Blackberry Wine	X	X	X			
The Imp's Delight	X	X	X			
Fish Cakes						

Continued on page 188

Continued from page 187

THE STORMLANDS & THE REACH	V	V+	GF	V*	V+*	GF*
Hunting Party Cakes	X					
Sweetmeats with Nuts and Honey	X					
Westerosi Strongwine	X	X	X			
Born Amidst Salt & Smoke			X			
Harvest Apple Tart	X					
Stuffed Figs	X		X			
Queen of Thorns Cheese Tart	X					
Citadel Soup	X				X	X
Arbor Gold	X	X	X			
Highgarden Lemon Cakes	X					

DORNE	V	V+	GF	V*	V+*	GF*
Spiced Orange Salad	X		X		X	
Lemon and Goat Cheese Dip	X		X			
Dornish Cheese and Pepper Pie	X					
Grilled Peaches	X		X		X	
Sunspear Soup	X	X	X			
Candied Plums	X		X		X	
Dornish Red	X	X	X			

ACROSS THE NARROW SEA	V	V+	GF	V*	V+*	GF*
Roasted Lamb			X			
Rizmon Mālor (Sand Rice)	X	X				
Drogon's Flame-Grilled Fish			X			
Khaleesi's Supper			X			
Tyroshi Pear Brandy	X		X		X	
Shade of the Evening	X	X	X			
Dusk Rose Tea	X		X		X	
A Girl's Oysters with Vinegar			X			
Plum Cake	X					

MEASUREMENT CONVERSIONS

VOLUME

US	METRIC
⅓ teaspoon (tsp)	1 mL
1 teaspoon (tsp)	5 mL
1 tablespoon (tbsp)	15 mL
1 fluid ounce (fl. oz.)	30 mL
⅕ cup	50 mL
¼ cup	60 mL
⅔ cup	80 mL
3.4 fluid ounces (fl. oz.)	100 mL
½ cup	120 mL
⅓ cup	160 mL
¾ cup	180 mL
1 cup	240 mL
1 pint (2 cups)	480 mL
1 quart (4 cups)	.95 liter

WEIGHT

OUNCES	GRAMS
.5 ounce (oz.)	14 grams (g)
1 ounce (oz.)	28 grams (g)
¼ pound (lb.)	113 grams (g)
⅓ pound (lb.)	151 grams (g)
½ pound (lb.)	227 grams (g)
1 pound (lb.)	454 grams (g)

TEMPERATURES

FAHRENHEIT	CELSIUS
200°F	93°C
212°F	100°C
250°F	121°C
275°F	135°C
300°F	149°C
325°F	163°C
350°F	177°C
400°F	204°C
425°F	218°C
450°F	232°C
475°F	246°C
500°F	260°C

ABOUT THE AUTHORS

Joanne Bourne is a writer and prehistorian from Kent in southern England. Her book, *The Maps Book* (Lonely Planet Kids), was shortlisted for the 2024 Edward Stanford Children's Travel Book of the Year. Her nature memoir *Flint: A Lithic Love Letter* is published by Eye Books. She is a huge *Game of Thrones* and *House of the Dragon* fan and was thrilled to collaborate with Cassandra Reeder on this book.

Author Cassandra Reeder launched her blog The Geeky Chef in 2008, bringing fictional food and drinks from a vast array of fandoms into reality with simple and fun recipes. Since then, a series of cookbooks based on the trailblazing blog have been published, including *The Geeky Chef Cookbook*, *The Geeky Bartender Drinks*, and *The Video Game Chef*. When not conjuring up recipes for fictional food, Cassandra can be found perusing the food carts in Portland, Oregon, with her husband and two tiny geeks.

ACKNOWLEDGMENTS

Thank you to my helpers and recipe testers: Rolanda Conversino, Nico Teolis, Jessica and Wesley Garcia, and Amanda and Bryan Backur. You have my everlasting love and gratitude. May the light of the seven shine upon you all.

Thank you to Jo Bourne, for being the loveliest co-author I could ever hope for. My everlasting gratitude to my husband and children, whose love and support sustain me.

CASSANDRA REEDER

PO Box 3088
San Rafael, CA 94912
www.insighteditions.com

Find us on Facebook: www.facebook.com/InsightEditions
Follow us on Instagram: @insighteditions

ISBN: 979-8-88663-471-6
Gift ISBN: 979-8-88663-480-8
Exclusive ISBN: 979-8-88663-830-1

Publisher: Raoul Goff
SVP, Group Publisher: Vanessa Lopez
VP, Creative: Chrissy Kwasnik
VP, Manufacturing: Alix Nicholaeff
Editorial Director: Lia Brown
Art Director: Stuart Smith
Designer: Brooke McCullum
Editor: Stephen Fall
Editorial Assistant: Jennifer Pellman
Executive Project Editor: Maria Spano
Production Manager: Deena Hashem
Senior Production Manager, Subsidiary Rights: Lina s Palma-Temena
Photographer: Ted Thomas
Food and Prop Stylist: Elena Craig and August Craig
Assistant Food Stylists: Lauren Tedeschi and Patricia Parrish

REPLANTED PAPER

Insight Editions, in association with Roots of Peace, will plant two trees for each tree used in the manufacturing of this book. Roots of Peace is an internationally renowned humanitarian organization dedicated to eradicating land mines worldwide and converting war-torn lands into productive farms and wildlife habitats. Roots of Peace will plant two million fruit and nut trees in Afghanistan and provide farmers there with the skills and support necessary for sustainable land use.

Manufactured in China by Insight Editions

10 9 8 7 6 5 4 3 2 1